Doll Fashion Studio

Sew 20 Seasonal Outfits
for Your 18-Inch Doll

Joan Hinds

KRAUSE PUBLICATIONS
Cincinnati, Ohio

Table of Contents

winter

spring

summer

fall

Children love to play with dolls, and dressing them in new clothing is a big part of playtime. Today, girls' favorite type of clothing for their dolls are the styles that they wear themselves. This includes everything from dress-up fashions to sportswear and all styles in between.

I have designed this book to include patterns for all types of clothing for 18-inch dolls. Twenty outfits organized by the seasons have been designed with the preteen girl in mind. These outfits span activities that girls participate in, such as school, extracurricular arts, outdoor activities and dress-up occasions.

Today's styles for girls combine many different prints for a look unique to their generation. Ruffled and gathered sleeves are back in style, as are gathered skirts. Dress-up clothes are almost always short-sleeved or sleeveless. Jackets and skirts are often seen with ruffles, too. You will find many of these fashion trends in the doll clothing designs in this book.

Be sure to visit the website listed for each outfit to see a video of a 360-degree view of the design.

Emily enjoys going outside whenever she can—snow or shine! She likes learning about the environment and enjoying the fresh air with her dog, Buddy. With a wardrobe as spirited and versatile as she is, this nature lover is always prepared for her next outdoor adventure!

Always full of energy, Chloe is an avid gymnast and soccer player. She may have just moved into town, but she already feels at home with her new friends. She loves to collect stuffed animals, and she never passes up an opportunity to wear something fun and comfortable.

Meet the Dolls

Welcome to Doll Fashion Studio! First, let's meet a group of very special girls as they dress to impress for a year of fun adventures and special occasions. These five best friends may be as different as can be, but their friendship—and sense of style—is second to none!

Lauren can usually be found with her nose in a book, reading and dreaming of far away places and imaginary worlds. It's a good thing she takes dance lessons with her friends to bring her down to Earth! Dressing up or dressing down is easy for this creative bookworm.

Playing her flute and singing in her school choir are Katy's favorite pastimes. She loves picking out the perfect dress to wear when she performs in front of her audiences or attends a party with her friends. Appearing polished and put-together are musts for Katy!

Sewing and crafting are Anna's favorite hobbies, especially making clothes for her doll. She loves to celebrate, and she is always prepared for holidays and sleepovers with her friends. Whether she's the hostess or the life of the party, Anna makes sure that she looks her best.

Chapter 1

Getting Started

This chapter will assist you in achieving the perfect fit for your doll clothing. If you are using a doll other than the American Girl® doll, tips are given to help you achieve a perfect fit.

All of the projects in this book use only basic sewing techniques. A few of the unusual methods are explained to insure sewing success. You probably have most of the tools needed, such as a sewing machine with a zigzag stitch, iron, pressing board, scissors, pins, etc. Other necessary supplies can be easily purchased at sewing and craft stores.

Advice is given to make fabric choices easier. Sewing such small doll garments requires that the fabric be lightweight. Bright floral prints are both stylish and popular with girls today. Choose the colors and prints that both you and your doll owner prefer to make each outfit unique.

Which Dolls Do These Patterns Fit?

The American Girl doll by Pleasant Company took the doll market by storm in the 1980s. With this rebirth of childlike play dolls, other manufacturers created their own brand of "18-inch (45.7cm) vinyl child dolls." The faces are all unique, but the cloth bodies are sufficiently similar to exchange clothing, particularly dresses. Arms and legs sometimes vary enough to require different sleeve and pant lengths, but most of the dolls can wear the clothing in this book.

Even within a single brand, stuffed cloth bodies may vary from doll to doll. The bodies don't come from a mold, and there is a human element involved in creating their fullness. Also, dolls that remain in stands or are actively played with may become slimmer over time. In most cases, the most critical measurement is the waist. The patterns in this book presume an 11" (27.9cm) waist. This measurement is most important when making garments with a waistband. If your doll comes from another manufacturer, you must take careful measurements before you start. Often the bodies will be slightly thinner, especially in the neckline and waist. Newer American Girl dolls may have slightly slimmer vinyl arms and legs, but that should not have an impact on the basic styles featured in the book. As long as this type of doll remains popular, more brands will appear each year. Be aware that the patterns may need slight adjustments in waistbands, hem and sleeve lengths, etc.

The clothing in the book was designed to fit the American Girl doll. You only need to have the waist measurement before sewing because it may vary. If you have another brand of doll, the best way to ensure a perfect fit for your particular doll is to also make a trial muslin for at least the bodice. This way you can accurately see how well the garment will fit. It is helpful if you have the doll you are sewing for in your possession while you make her clothing. Try each garment on the doll as you are sewing to make sure you have the proper fit.

Because the clothing in this book has been designed for American Girl dolls, I will give you a few tips to adjust the patterns. If your doll is slimmer, you will probably need to adjust the waist. If the garment has elastic in the waistband, you can shorten the elastic length to make it fit. You can overlap the center back edges of the bodice before you sew the Velcro® in place if the top is slightly larger than you would like. If the bodice or shirt is quite full, take a small amount off the side seams or the center back seam before finishing the garment.

Most dolls will not have a waist thicker than 11" (27.9cm) around. If you need to add width to the clothing, adding a small amount to the side seams under the armholes will usually suffice. To widen pants at the waist, add a small amount to the width at the top of the pants pattern pieces, and be sure to lengthen the waistband.

Tools and Equipment

Gather all your tools and equipment before you begin. Start with a basic sewing machine. It should be capable of making straight and zigzag stitches. Some of the specialty feet you may find helpful are an edgestitching foot and a zipper foot. The edgestitching foot has a metal guide along one side of the presser foot. This guide lines up along the fabric edge and will ensure a straight stitching line. It can also provide you with an accurate ¼" (6mm) seam allowance for doll clothing. And, obviously, the zipper foot will assist with zipper insertions. Make sure your machine is stocked with new needles appropriate for your fabric choices. A serger is not necessary, even for the knit T-shirts, but it helps with construction and gives seam allowances a clean finish. If you don't have a serger, finish the seams with a zigzag stitch. Another choice is to cut out the garment with pinking shears, which will finish the seam as well.

A steam iron is a must. There is a "mini-iron" designed for the quilting industry that is also perfect for the small areas in doll clothing construction. Small ironing boards or sleeve pressing boards are wonderful for pressing small sleeves, collars, pant legs, etc. Use a metal hem gauge to achieve a straight line when pressing fabric edges to the wrong side. A large ironing board may not be necessary. Try using a small board or flat mat to press your projects.

Rotary cutters, mats and rulers make cutting your fabric quick and easy. Use them to cut all the straight pattern pieces that have only measurements given. Be sure to have a sharp blade to limit frustration when cutting.

Other tools needed are the usual items found in sewing kits, including sewing shears, small clippers, straight pins, seam gauge, tape measure and wash-out marker. If you are going to work the hand embroidery, you will need a sharp embroidery scissors and crewel needles. Temporary spray adhesive, a bodkin for inserting elastic, a fabric tube turner or bodkin with a latch, pinking shears and bias tape makers will also come in handy.

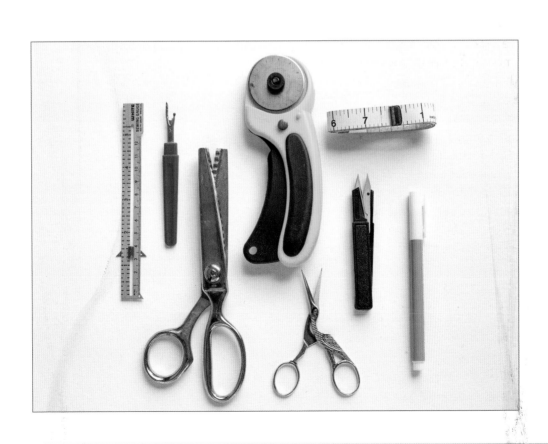

Sewing Basics

The skills needed for the projects in the book are not complicated. Basic techniques of garment construction are used along with a few tips of my own. Please note that the seam allowance is ¼" (6mm) unless noted otherwise in the instructions.

Back Openings

In most cases the back of the garment is open all the way for easier dressing. You can choose how to close the garments. The most common way is with a hook-and-loop closure such as Velcro, but substitute small snaps if you prefer. Facings are difficult to apply to doll garments because the pieces are so small. I like to use a self lining in bodices of dresses or tops, which is described in the project instructions.

Sewing With Knits

Sewing with knits only requires a few minor changes. Make sure your sewing machine needle is appropriate for knits. The seams in the knit garments are quite short, which helps eliminate stretching. Use a straight or zigzag stitch if using your sewing machine, or stitch the seams with a serger. You may want to try a double needle for hems on the shirts and leggings.

Seam Finishes

Seam finishes are your choice. Common methods are serging, zigzag stitching or using pinking shears. A serged seam finish will look the most like ready-to-wear clothing. Zigzag stitching will prevent raveled seams as well. I have included the phrase "serge or zigzag stitch" when I feel a seam finish is necessary. Pinking shears are often used with doll clothing seams. They can be used to trim the seam around curves so clipping the seam will not be necessary. If you like, you can even cut out the doll pattern pieces with pinking shears to eliminate any trimming later.

Gathers

To make gathers on skirts or ruffles, place the fabric under the presser foot on the stitching line about a seam width away from the edge. Turn the wheel by hand to take one stitch. Pull up on the top thread and bring the bobbin thread to the top of the fabric. Pull both of the threads together to the length of the area to be gathered. Place them under the presser foot after giving them a gentle twist. Now adjust your machine for a medium zigzag stitch with a length of about 3.0. Stitch across the threads just inside the seam allowance, making sure not to stitch directly on the threads (Gathers 1). Stop a seam width away from the edge. Pull on the twisted threads to gather the fabric. Because the threads were secured in the beginning, they will not come out. Secure the thread tails by wrapping them around a pin after the gathers are pulled to the correct size (Gathers 2).

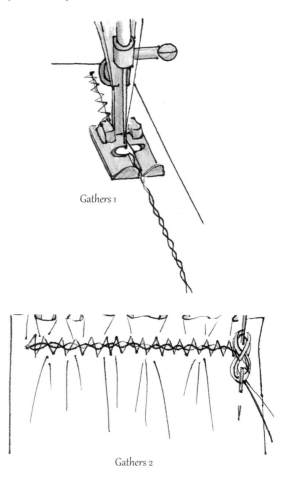

Gathers 1

Gathers 2

Straps

An important technique to learn is making straps for the garments. Straps often need a little support, and this technique provides a type of interfacing made from the seam allowance. First the strap should be cut three times the finished width dimension. This has already been calculated for you in the instructions in the book.

With right sides together, sew the length of the strap with a ¼" (6mm) seam allowance (Straps 1). Press the seam allowance open by using a metal tube inserted in the strap or by using the point of the iron. Turn the strap right side out, using a fabric tube turner or a bodkin with a latch. Press the strap flat by centering the seam. Note that the seam allowances inside the strap extend to the folded edges to give it extra body (Straps 2).

Straps 1

Straps 2

Bias Bindings and Straps

When making bias bindings and straps, use a bias tape maker to press the cut edges. Fold them again and press. If the bias strip will be applied to a curved surface, press that part of the bias strip to form a curve, which will make it easier to apply.

Fabric Choices

Now for the fun part—choosing fabrics! Many of the garments and accessories have been made from cotton fabrics. Many cotton prints today are designed to have several companion prints. These make bright, colorful clothes that girls love. For fabrics other than cottons, the weight of the fabric is important. Making denim skirts and shorts for dolls is much easier and they fit better if the denim is lightweight. Another substitute for denim would be a chambray or lightweight twill. Remember that satin and other shiny fabrics will slip, so pin often. Knits are very popular and can be used for more than T-shirts. If you choose to use laminated cotton for the raincoat—fabric with a flexible protective finish applied to the surface—follow these tips to make sewing easier:

- Only put pins inside the seam allowance when cutting and sewing your fabric. Pins will leave a permanent mark on the fabric. Try using double-sided or cellophane tape to hold the fabrics together when cutting and sewing.
- Do not press the fabric from the right side because the coating on the fabric will melt. Press only if needed on the wrong side or on the lining side.
- Use a sharp needle, size 12, with a ⅛" (3mm) stitch length. If needed, try a Teflon-coated presser foot when topstitching to keep the foot from sticking.

Often the perfect fabric is not available at your local fabric store. In this case, look at children's ready-mades! I found the perfect matching ribbing for the hoodie (page 82) on a boy's sweatshirt that was marked down for clearance. I have enough to make three or four more. The summer PJs top (page 70) was cut from a girl's T-shirt because it was such an adorable print. I used the bottom of the shirt to make the ruffle, so I didn't have to stitch a hem—it was done for me. Use any fabric and trim choices available. You never know how wonderful the results will be!

Chapter 2

Winter Fashion

Wintertime brings exciting holiday celebrations, the taste of snowflakes on your tongue and enjoying a cup of hot chocolate in your favorite nightgown with your best friend. Make new doll fashions for the season from this assortment of outfits.

For casual wear, the *School Picture Day Outfit* (page 14) fills the bill. The skirt has a circular ruffle and elastic in the back waistband. The fabric I chose is denim with a shiny multicolor print, but a solid color will work as well. The tank top is unique with lingerie elastic at the top edges and armholes, making for easy construction. The shrug is made from a sweater knit fabric to give it texture. The front ties are made separately and attached to the front opening.

Dolls will want to spend lots of time outdoors in their *Snow Day Outfit* (page 20). The jacket, made from suede cloth, is gathered below the yoke. The separating zipper is easy to apply with basting tape. The pants are made from a heavy knit fabric with elastic at the waist. Use sweatshirt fleece with a cotton lining for the cap and mittens. The face is made from felt, and the whiskers are simple hand embroidery stitches. The mittens have ribbing at the top to hold them on her hands. Change the shape of the ears to make different animal faces.

The *Sweet Valentine Dress* (page 26) has a large heart pocket on the skirt to hold tiny doll-sized valentines. Use a charming heart-print cotton fabric and a matching solid fabric for the bands on the neckline, waist and skirt.

The *Snowy Nightgown* (page 32) is just right for sleepovers or reading a good book. Choose a warm flannel print or a flannel-backed satin. The pleats in the front and back are simple to make. The easy construction of the nightgown includes a Velcro closure.

Every girl wants a beautiful holiday dress. The *Elegant Holiday Dress* (page 36) is made from velvet and a sheer organza overskirt. The underskirt is a circle skirt made of a crisp fabric such as taffeta to give the skirt body. The small cap sleeves have a ruffle over the sleeve cap. The sash with a purchased ribbon rose is attached to the dress with a separate bow at the back.

Two projects in this chapter that you can make with a doll's young owner are *Valentines* (page 30) and a stuffed *Teddy Bear* (page 35). The valentines are cut from cardstock and decorated with stickers. The bear is made of felt and uses hand-embroidery stitches. To make the project simpler, use a fine-point permanent marker to draw the face. This project will require more assistance from an adult, but it is a good way to learn hand-sewing and embroidery techniques.

School Picture Day Outfit

Anna spent all morning picking out the perfect skirt, tank top and shrug for picture day at her school. She loves to practice her smile in the mirror and swap her finished photos with her friends.

See a 360-degree view of this outfit here: www.marthapullen.com/doll-fashion-studio.html

SUPPLIES:

SKIRT
- Patterns No. 1, No. 2, No. 3, No. 4
- ¼ yd. (22.9cm) lightweight denim or twill
- 4½" (11.4cm) elastic, ¼" (6mm) wide

TANK TOP
- Patterns No. 5, No. 6
- ¼ yd. (22.9cm) knit fabric
- ¾ yd. (68.6cm) decorative stretch lace, ½"(13mm) wide
- 2½" (6.4cm) Velcro strip, cut in half

SHRUG
- Patterns No. 7, No. 8, No. 9
- ¼ yd. (22.9cm) sweater knit fabric

Skirt

1 Cut two fronts, two backs, one front ruffle, one back ruffle and a waistband measuring 1½" × 14¼" (3.8cm × 36.2cm).

2 With right sides together, sew the center front and center back seams and press (Skirt 1). Surge or zigzag stitch the lower edge of each ruffle. Press the edges ¼" (6mm) to the wrong side and stitch. Sew the front ruffle to the bottom of the front skirt with right sides together (Skirt 2). Serge or zigzag the seam allowances and press them toward the skirt. Topstitch along the seam line. Repeat with the back skirt and back ruffle.

3 With right sides together, stitch the side seams of the skirt, including the ruffle, and press.

4 Serge or zigzag stitch along one edge of the waistband. With right sides together, sew the short ends and press the seam allowances open. Sew the unfinished edge of the waistband to the skirt with right sides together, matching the waistband seam to the center back seam of the skirt. Fold the waistband over to the inside of the skirt so the waistband is ½" (13mm) wide. Topstitch in place, leaving a 1" (2.5cm) opening at each side seam for the casing (Skirt 3).

5 Thread the elastic through the back waistband and secure at each side seam. Stitch the openings in the waistband closed.

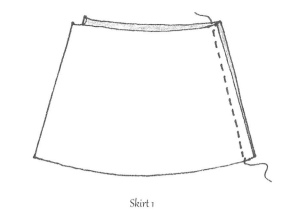

Skirt 1

Skirt 2

Skirt 3

Tank Top

1 Cut one front and two backs from the knit fabric.

2 Cut a 4" (10.2cm) piece of stretch lace for the top edge of the front. Place the stretch lace on the right side of the top so that the stretch lace extends slightly above the cut edge and zigzag stitch (Tank 1).

3 Cut 2½" (6.4cm) of stretch lace for the top edge of each back. Stitch to the backs in the same manner as the front. Press the center back edges ¼" (6mm) to the wrong side and stitch (Tank 2)

4 Cut a 9" (22.9cm) piece of stretch lace for each armhole. Begin stitching the stretch lace to the front armhole, covering the cut end of the stretch lace across the top. Mark the stretch lace 2¾" (7.0cm) away from the top edge and begin stitching the remaining stretch lace to the back armhole. Repeat with the other armhole (Tank 3).

5 Sew the side seams with right sides together (Tank 4). Serge or zigzag stitch the lower edge of the top and press ¼" (6mm) to the wrong side. Topstitch.

6 Lapping right over left, sew the Velcro to the back opening.

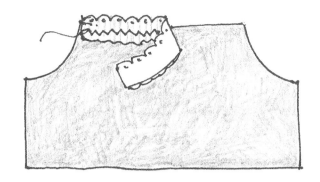

Tank 1

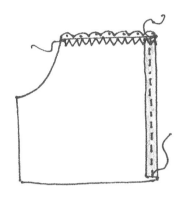

Tank 2

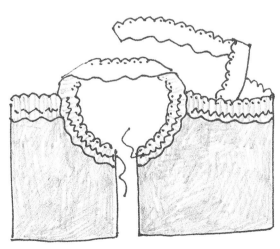

Tank 3

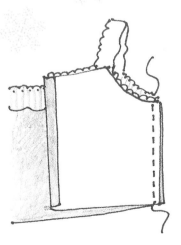

Tank 4

Shrug

1 Cut two fronts, one back, two sleeves and a strip 1½" × 8" (3.8cm × 20.3cm).

2 With right sides together, sew the shoulder seams of the front and the back using a zigzag stitch or a serged seam. Press the seam allowances to the back.

3 Press the center front edges and back neckline ¼" (6mm) to the wrong side and topstitch with a zigzag stitch. Press the lower edges of each front and back ¼" (6mm) to the wrong side and topstitch as above (Shrug 1).

4 Press the lower edges of each sleeve ¼" (6mm) to the wrong side and topstitch with a zigzag stitch. With right sides together, sew the sleeve caps to the armholes, easing to fit. The sleeve caps are full, but the armholes can be stretched slightly to fit. Sew the underarm seam (Shrug 2).

5 Press one long edge of the strip ½" (13mm) to the wrong side. Press the other long edge ½" (13mm) to the wrong side. (The edges will overlap each other.) Using a wide zigzag stitch, sew down the center of the strip to cover the raw edges (Shrug 3). Cut the strip in half widthwise. Fold one end of each tie ¼" (6mm) to the wrong side and stitch with a straight stitch. Place the raw end of each tie ½" (13mm) under the point in each center front and stitch with a zigzag stitch to secure (Shrug 4).

6 When the shrug is worn, tie a knot with the strips in the front.

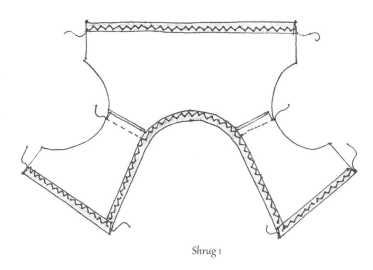

Shrug 1

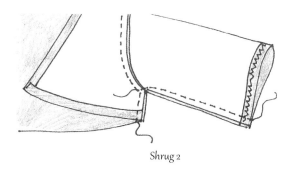

Shrug 2

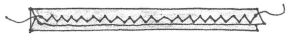

Shrug 3

Shrug 4

Doll Fashion Tip

The Shrug is a very popular style for girls today. Sweater knits can be found in most major fabric stores. If you prefer, try using another knit fabric. Substitute ribbons for the ties to create an even easier project.

Snow Day Outfit

SUPPLIES:

JACKET AND PANTS

- Patterns No. 10, No. 11, No. 12, No. 13 (for jacket)
- Pattern No. 14 (for pants)
- ¼ yd. (22.9cm) suede cloth fabric
- 5" (12.7cm) separating zipper
- Narrow double-sided adhesive basting tape
- 8" (20.3cm) single fold bias tape
- ⅓ yd. (30.5cm) solid knit fabric (for pants)
- 10" (25.4cm) decorative or lingerie elastic, ½" (13mm) wide

KITTY CAP AND MITTENS

- Pattern No. 15 (for cap)
- Pattern No. 16 (for mittens)
- Pattern pieces labeled Kitty Cap Ear, Cap Nose, Mitten Ear, and Mitten Nose
- ¼ yd. (22.9cm) sweatshirt fleece fabric
- Fat quarter of pink cotton fabric (for lining)
- Scrap of pink felt (for ears and nose)
- 2 buttons, size ½" (13mm)
- 1 skein white embroidery floss
- ½ yd. (45.7cm) white cord, ⅜" (10mm) thick
- 2 pompoms, size 1" (2.5cm)
- 1¼" × 7" (3.2cm × 17.8cm) piece of white ribbing
- 2 buttons, size ¼" (6mm)
- Fabric glue

See a 360-degree view of this outfit here: www.marthapullen.com/doll-fashion-studio.html

For Emily, nothing is better than a snow day! Her cap and mittens keep her toasty warm as she builds the first snowman of the season and plays in piles of snow with her dog, Buddy.

Jacket

1 Cut two upper fronts and one upper back, two sleeves, one collar, two lower fronts 3¼" × 6" (8.3cm × 15.2cm) and one lower back 3¼" × 12" (8.3cm × 30.5cm) from the suede cloth.

2 Serge or zigzag stitch one long edge of both lower fronts and the lower back. Press ¼" (6mm) to the wrong side and stitch.

3 Gather the remaining long edges of the lower fronts and the lower back. With right sides together, sew the lower fronts to the upper fronts and the lower back to the upper back (Jacket 1).

4 With right sides together, sew the upper back to the upper fronts at the shoulders and press.

Jacket 1

Jacket 2

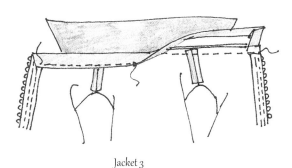

Jacket 3

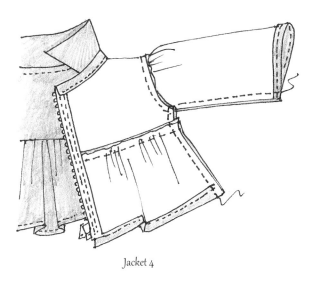

Jacket 4

5 Cut a piece of the basting tape the length of the zipper and peel off the backing. Apply to one side of the zipper and remove the paper on the top. Place this half of the zipper along the front opening with the bottom of the zipper placed ⅛" (3mm) from the lower edge of the jacket. Stitch the zipper ¼" (6mm) from the front edge using a zipper foot. Open out the zipper to the right side and pin ¼" (6mm) from the stitched seam. Stitch using a zipper or edge-stitching presser foot. Stitch the other half of the zipper to the remaining front edge in the same manner (Jacket 2).

6 Fold the collar in half with right sides together. Stitch the ends and turn to the right side. Press. Center the cut edges of the collar on the neckline and stitch. Note that the collar does not come all the way to the center front edges. Stitch the bias tape to the neckline, extending the ends by ¼" (6mm). Cut off the excess. Turn the bias tape to the inside and pin to the jacket, tucking in the short ends. Stitch (Jacket 3).

7 Serge or zigzag stitch the lower edges of the sleeves. Press them ¼" (6mm) to the wrong side and stitch. Gather the sleeve caps and stitch to the armholes with right sides together. Sew the underarm seams from the sleeve edges to the bottom of the jacket (Jacket 4).

Pants

1 Cut two pants from the knit fabric. With right sides together, sew the pants along the center front seam and press (Pants 1).

2 Place one end of the elastic at the center back, overlapping the top edge of the pants. Pull the elastic to the other side while zigzag stitching it in place (Pants 2).

3 Press the lower leg edges ¼" (6mm) to the wrong side and topstitch. Sew the center back seam with right sides together.

4 Sew the inner leg seam (Pants 3).

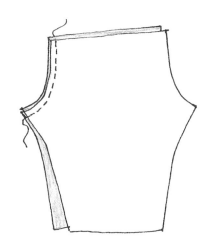

Pants 1

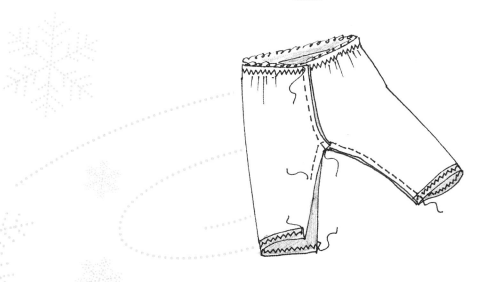

Pants 2

Pants 3

Kitty Cap

1 Cut one cap from the sweatshirt fleece fabric and one from the lining fabric. Cut two ears and one nose from the felt.

2 With right sides together, sew the center back seam of the cap. Do the same with the lining. Press the seam allowances open (Cap 1).

3 Cut the cord in half. Sew a pompom at one end of each piece.

4 Pin the raw ends of the cords on the seam line of the cap as marked on the pattern piece (Cap 2). Place the cap and lining with right sides together and stitch around the face and lower edges of the cap, making sure not to catch the other ends of the cords in the stitching. Clip the curves and turn to the right side. Press (Cap 3).

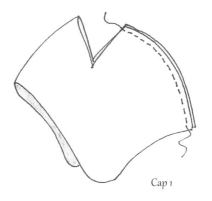

Cap 1

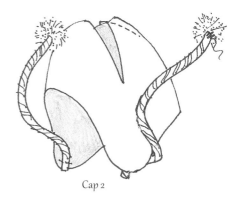

Cap 2

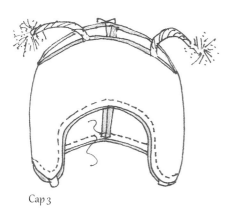

Cap 3

5 Treating the cap and lining as one, stitch the dart in the front of the cap. Pin the remaining raw edges together with the bottom edges of the ears placed along the seam allowance as marked on the pattern piece. Match the dart to the center back seam and stitch (Cap 4).

6 Sew the ½" (13mm) buttons to the cap as marked on the pattern piece. Glue the nose to the cap. Using a stem stitch, hand embroider the whiskers with three strands of floss (Cap 5).

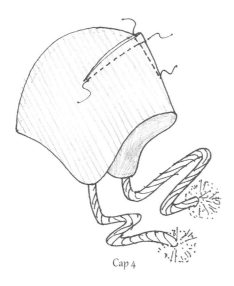

Cap 4

Cap 5

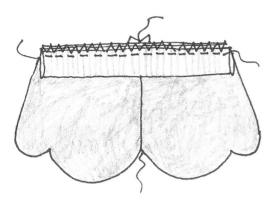

Mittens 1

Kitty Mittens

1 Cut four mittens from the sweatshirt fleece. Cut four ears and two noses from the felt.

2 With right sides together, stitch two mittens together up to the dot marked on the pattern piece. Open out flat.

3 Cut the ribbing in half widthwise. Fold the ribbing in half lengthwise with wrong sides together so it will measure $\frac{5}{8}$" (16mm) in width. Pin the ribbing to the right side of the mittens along the straight edges. Zigzag stitch or serge (Mittens 1).

4 Fold the mittens with right sides together and finish stitching the seam from the dot to the thumb end. Clip the curves and turn to the right side (Mittens 2).

5 Sew the $\frac{1}{4}$" (6mm) buttons to the mittens as marked on the pattern piece. Glue the ears and noses to the mittens. Work three long straight stitches with three strands of embroidery floss on both sides of each nose (Mittens 3).

Mittens 2

Mittens 3

Sweet Valentine Dress

Valentine's Day is even more special when Lauren wears her heart-print dress. She loves to hand out valentines at school that she keeps hidden in her heart-shaped pocket. Help her make more for her friends!

See a 360-degree view of this outfit here: www.marthapullen.com/doll-fashion-studio.html

SUPPLIES:

DRESS

- Patterns No. 17, No. 18, No. 19, No. 20, No. 21, No. 22
- ⅓ yd. (30.5cm) print fabric
- ⅓ yd. (30.5cm) contrasting fabric
- 3" (7.6cm) Velcro strip, cut in half

VALENTINES

- Cardstock
- Assorted Valentine stickers
- Fine-point marker

Dress

1 Cut one front bodice, two back bodices, two sleeves and one skirt 4¼" × 36" (10.8cm × 91.4cm) from the print fabric. Cut one front neck band, two back neck bands, one front bodice, two back bodices, two sleeve bands 1¼" × 5" (3.2cm × 12.7cm), two pockets, one waistband 1¼" × 13¼" (3.2cm × 33.7cm), and one skirt band 3½" × 36" (8.9cm × 91.4cm) from the contrasting fabric.

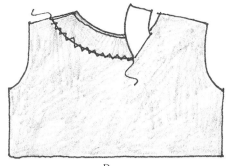

Dress 1

2 Place the wrong side of the front neck band and the back neck bands on the right side of the bodice front and backs so the neck bands are flush. Stitch the bands on the bodice pieces around the outer edge with a narrow zigzag stitch (Dress 1).

3 With right sides together, sew the shoulder seams of the front and backs with the bands. Press the seam allowances open. Repeat with the remaining bodice pieces for the lining. Sew the bodice to the lining around the neckline and the center backs (Dress 2). With right sides together, clip the curves and corners and turn to the right side. Press.

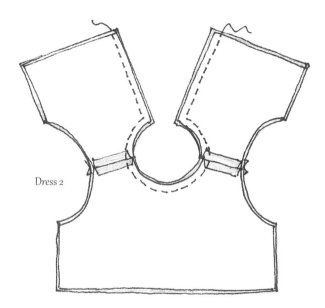

Dress 2

4 Gather the top and bottom edges of the sleeves. Press one long edge of the sleeve bands ¼" (6mm) to the wrong side. With the right side of the unpressed edge of the sleeve band to the wrong side of the sleeve, sew the band to the sleeve (Dress 3). Fold the band over the seam allowance to the front and topstitch. Press. Sew the sleeve cap to the armhole with right sides together. Sew the underarm seam (Dress 4).

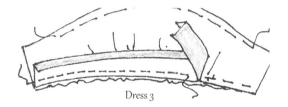

Dress 3

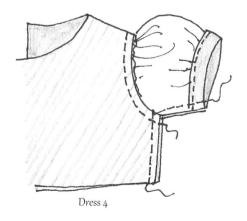

Dress 4

5 Press the ends of the waistband ¼" (6mm) to the wrong side and stitch. Sew the band to the bottom of the bodice with right sides together. Serge or zigzag stitch the seam allowance to finish (Dress 5).

6 Fold the skirt band in half lengthwise and press. Sew the band to one long edge of the skirt with right sides together. Serge or zigzag stitch the side edges and press them ¼" (6mm) to the wrong side. Stitch (Dress 6).

7 With right sides together, sew the pockets, leaving a small opening for turning along one side (Dress 7). Clip the curves and turn to the right side. Press, folding the unstitched part to the inside. Place the pocket on the skirt 2" (5.1cm) from the lower edge and 1½" (3.8cm) from the center. Stitch the sides of the pocket to the skirt so the top of the heart is open (Dress 8).

8 Gather the top edge of the skirt and stitch it to the waistband with right sides together. Serge or zigzag stitch the seam allowance to finish.

9 Lapping right over left, sew the Velcro to the back opening.

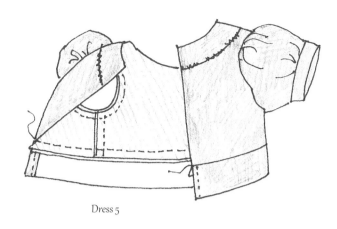

Dress 5

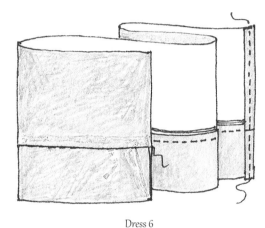

Dress 6

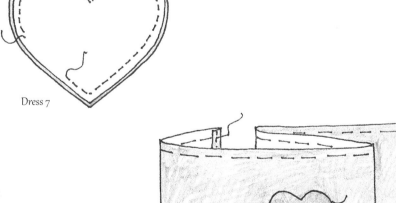

Dress 7

Dress 8

My Doll's Valentines

a project to make together!

Heart-Shaped Valentine

1 Cut a piece of cardstock 1½" × 2½" (3.8cm × 6.4cm) and fold in half to make a 1¼" × 1½" (3.2cm × 3.8cm) card. With a pencil, draw a heart with the top of the heart along the fold. Cut out the heart, making sure that the top of the heart is not cut. This will give a back to the heart card (Card 1).

2 Place a foam heart sticker on the front with a smaller heart sticker in the center. Write a phrase on the inside such as "Luv ya!" and add small hearts if desired.

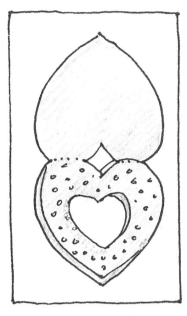

Card 1

Card 2

Rectangular Valentine

1 Cut a rectangle 1½" × 2½" (3.8cm × 6.4cm) and fold in half as above.

2 Place stickers on the front. Write a desired phrase on the inside such as "Be Mine." Add small hearts if desired (Card 2).

Snowy Nightgown

Chloe loves this warm and cuddly flannel nightgown—it's as soft as her teddy bear! She wears it on cold winter evenings after a cup of hot cocoa or to one of Anna's many winter sleepovers.

See a 360-degree view of this outfit here: www.marthapullen.com/doll-fashion-studio.html

SUPPLIES:

GOWN

- Patterns No. 23, No. 24, No. 25, No. 26, No. 27
- ½ yd. (45.7cm) flannel
- 3" (7.6cm) Velcro strip, cut in half

TEDDY BEAR

- Pattern No. 28 and Teddy Bear Nose
- 4" × 6" (10.2cm × 15.2cm) piece of felt
- Scrap of white felt
- 2 skeins embroidery floss, one black and one additional color
- Crewel hand sewing needle, size 7
- Polyester stuffing
- Pencil or fabric marker
- Small ribbon bow

Gown

1 Cut two fronts, four backs, two sleeves, one front skirt, two back skirts and two bias strips 1¼" × 5" (3.2cm × 12.7cm).

2 With right sides together, sew one front to two backs at the shoulders. Press the seam allowances open. Repeat with the remaining pieces for the lining.

3 Sew the lining to the nightgown with right sides together around the neckline and up each center back (Gown 1). Clip the corners and curves. Turn to the right side and press.

4 Make the pleats in the front nightgown skirt. Find the center front and fold the first mark to the right toward the second one as marked on the pattern piece. Pin. Fold the next one as marked on the pattern piece. Repeat with the two pleats on the left. Baste at the top. Stitch the skirt to the front with right sides together and serge or zigzag stitch the seam allowances (Gown 2).

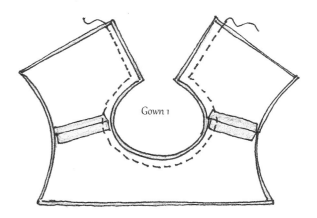

Gown 1

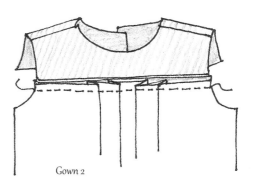

Gown 2

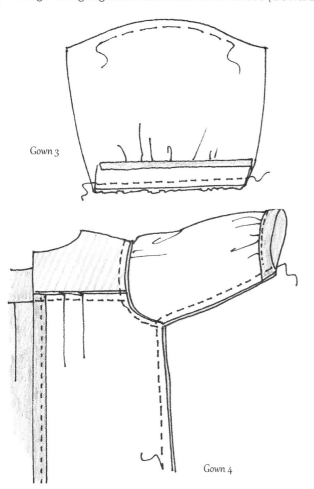

Gown 3

Gown 4

5 Serge or zigzag stitch the center back edges of the back skirts. Press ¼" (6mm) to the wrong side and stitch. Make the pleats as above in the back skirts as marked on the pattern piece. The pleats on the right side are folded to the right, and the pleats on the left are folded toward the left. Baste. With right sides together, sew the skirts to the backs. Serge or zigzag stitch the seam allowances.

6 Gather the lower edge of the sleeves. Press one long edge of the bias strips ¼" (6mm) to the wrong side. Sew the right side of the unpressed edges to the wrong side of the sleeves (Gown 3). Fold the strips to the right side and topstitch.

7 Gather the sleeve caps and stitch them to the arm-holes. With right sides together, sew the underarm seam from the sleeve edge to the bottom of the skirt (Gown 4).

8 Serge or zigzag stitch the hem of the nightgown and press it ½" (13mm) to the wrong side. Topstitch.

9 Lapping right over left, sew the Velcro to the center back opening.

My Doll's Teddy Bear

1 Fold the felt in half and trace the bear shape with a fabric marker or pencil. Cut out two bears.

2 Trace one nose on the white felt, but don't cut it out. Thread the needle with two strands of black floss no longer than 18" (45.7cm) in length and tie a knot. With a pencil or marker, draw the nose and mouth lines. Make several straight stitches in one place for the nose. Make one straight stitch for the line from the nose to the mouth and two straight stitches for the mouth (Bear 1). Cut out the nose and tack it to the bear's face. Make several straight stitches in place on the bear for each eye.

3 Cut three strands of floss in the contrasting color no longer than 18" (45.7cm) and thread the needle. Tie a knot. Bring the needle up from the back of the top side of the bear at his left arm. Place the two bear shapes wrong sides together. The knot will be hidden between the layers of the bear. Begin making a running stitch along the outside of the bear about ⅛" (3mm) from the edge. The stitches should be about ⅛" (3mm) long (Bear 2).

4 When you reach the other arm, stop the stitching and stuff the bear lightly with the polyester stuffing. Pin the bear closed and continue making a running stitch. When you reach the beginning point, make a couple of stitches in place to secure the thread.

5 Tack the bow to the upper left ear if desired.

Bear 1

Bear 2

a project to make together!

Elegant Holiday Dress

Winter holiday parties require a beautiful and elegant outfit—and Katy has just the thing! She feels like a princess when she wears her ruby red dress and twirls on her toes to an enchanting song.

See a 360-degree view of this outfit here: www.marthapullen.com/doll-fashion-studio.html

SUPPLIES:

- Patterns No. 29, No. 30, No. 31, No. 32, No. 33, No. 34, No. 35
- ¼ yd. (22.9cm) velvet or velveteen (for bodice)
- ½ yd. (45.7cm) taffeta (for underskirt)
- ⅓ yd. (30.5cm) sheer fabric, such as organza (for overskirt)
- Purchased ribbon rose, 2" (5.1cm) in diameter
- 3" (7.6cm) Velcro strip, cut in half

Dress

Note: Remember to press velvet only from the back of the fabric to prevent damaging the nap. If you prefer, substitute a satin or cotton print for the velvet.

1 Cut one front, two backs, two sleeves, two sleeve ruffles and one bias strip 1" × 10" (2.5cm × 25.4cm) from the velvet. Cut one front skirt, two back skirts, one sash and one bow 2½" × 22" (6.4cm × 55.9cm) from the taffeta. Cut one overskirt 8½" × 29" (21.6cm × 73.7cm) from the sheer fabric.

2 With right sides together, sew the shoulder seams of the bodice front and backs. Serge or zigzag stitch the center backs and press ¼" (6mm) to the wrong side. Stitch (Dress 1).

3 Serge or zigzag stitch one long edge of the bias strip. With right sides together, place the unpressed edge on the neckline and stitch. Fold the bias to the wrong side and topstitch on the right side "in the ditch" to secure the bias underneath (Dress 2).

4 Serge or zigzag stitch the lower edges of each sleeve and the longer straight edges of each sleeve ruffle. Press the edges ¼" (6mm) to the wrong side and topstitch (Dress 3).

5 Gather the unpressed edge of each sleeve ruffle to fit the sleeve caps (Dress 4). Place the wrong side of the ruffle over the right side of the sleeve cap and stitch to the armhole, easing to fit. Serge or zigzag the seam allowances. Topstitch along the bodice close to the armhole seam.

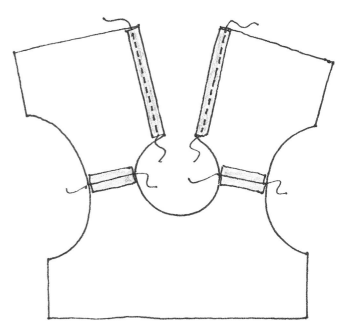

Dress 1

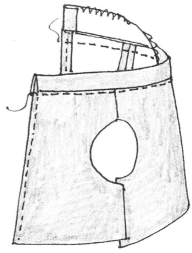

Dress 2

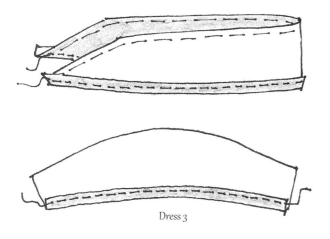

Dress 3

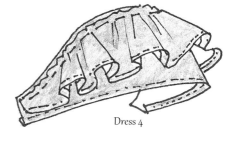

Dress 4

6 Sew the underarm seam from the sleeve edge to the lower edge of the bodice (Dress 5).

7 Fold the sash in half lengthwise with right sides together and stitch the short ends. Turn to the right side and press. Place the cut edges of the sash along the lower edge of the bodice and stitch, including the short ends (Dress 6).

8 With right sides together, sew the side seams of the taffeta skirt. Sew the center back seam to the dot marked on the pattern piece. Press the seam allowances open, including the unstitched part. Topstitch around the opening (Dress 7). Serge or zigzag stitch the lower edge of the skirt. Press it ¼" (6mm) to the wrong side and topstitch.

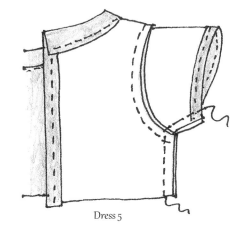

Dress 5

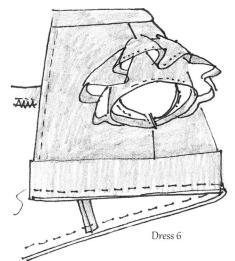

Dress 6

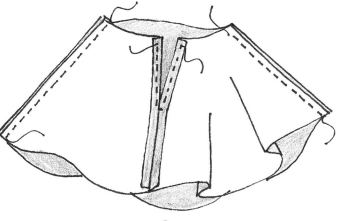

Dress 7

9 With right sides together, sew the sides of the over-skirt with a ½" (13mm) seam allowance to within 3" (7.6cm) from the top edge. Press the seam allowances ¼" (6mm) to the wrong side, including the unstitched part. Topstitch the length of the seam on both sides. This will prevent raveling (Dress 8).

10 Press the lower edge of the overskirt ½" (13mm) to the wrong side, and then another ½" (13mm). Topstitch. Gather the top of the overskirt to fit the taffeta skirt (Dress 9).

11 With right sides together, sew the skirts to the bodice.

12 Lapping right over left, sew the Velcro to the back opening. Press all the edges of the bow ¼" (6mm) to the wrong side. Press another ¼" (6mm) and stitch (Dress 10). Tie into a bow (Dress 11). Tack to the back opening on the right side. Tack the ribbon rose to the sash just slightly to the right of the center front.

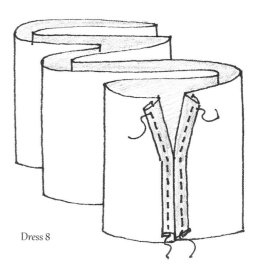

Dress 8

Dress 9

Dress 10

Dress 11

Doll Fashion Tip

Velvet is the perfect fabric for this elegant Holiday Dress. Be sure to turn the nap of the fabric so that it runs in the same direction on all of the pattern pieces. The bias strip can be easier to sew if you substitute taffeta for the bias strip. The end result will be just as beautiful.

Chapter 3

Spring Fashion

Warmer weather and colorful tulips announce the arrival of spring. Your doll can have a bright new wardrobe too. Recitals and graduations are highlights of the season. This chapter features outfits and accessories for springtime fun and celebrations.

The *Graduation Day Outfit* (page 44) features a cap and gown made of satin, but you can substitute a cotton fabric if you prefer. The gown has a long zipper in the front and pleats below the yokes in the front and the back. The cap is really quite simple because it has a stiff interfacing in the riser and the top. The cap top has two squares of satin sewn together, but one has a hole cut for the attachment of the band.

Spring holidays call for a *Special Occasion Dress*. This fancy dress (page 50) has princess styling and contrasting bands at the top and lower edges. The fabric is shiny polyester, but you could make the dress out of cotton, satin or taffeta. The straps and bows contrast in a darker fabric. The dress is open down the back to make it easy to dress a doll.

The *Spring Break Outfit* (page 54) is perfect for playing and traveling. Choose from wonderful matching cotton prints to make capri pants and a sleeveless top. The pants have contrasting fabric cuffs. The top is baby-doll style with a sleeveless yoke and a gathered lower ruffle. It can be worn with or without a T-shirt. The instructions for a short-sleeved T-shirt are included.

The sleeveless *Recital Dress* (page 60) has a unique style with a gathered upper bodice and bias strips for contrast. An easy gathered skirt is attached to the completed bodice.

Girls love to jump in puddles left by the spring rains. Dolls can do the same with the raglan-sleeved *Rainy Day Fashion Raincoat* (page 64). Use waterproof polyester or laminated cotton to give the raincoat a realistic look. It is lined with bright cotton, which is also used for the ruffles on the sleeves and hood. Matching decorative snaps serve as the closure.

The accessory projects to make together with the doll's owner are a paper *Diploma* (page 49) and a felt *Shoulder Purse* (page 59). The easy-to-make diploma is simply a rolled up tube of soft scrapbook paper tied with ribbon. Print your own message on the inside of the paper if you like. The purse is made by stitching embroidered felt together. Use ribbon for the strap. This project will need some adult supervision with the embroidery stitches.

Graduation Day Outfit

Emily is proud to wear her graduation gown and cap at the end of her school year as her family members congratulate her and her friends. All of them wonder what their next year in school has in store for them!

See a 360-degree view of this outfit here: www.marthapullen.com/doll-fashion-studio.html

SUPPLIES:

CAP AND GOWN

- Patterns No. 36, No. 37, No. 38 and Armhole Cutout (for gown)
- Patterns No. 39, No. 40 (for cap)
- 1 yd. (91.4cm) satin fabric
- 10" (25.4cm) separating zipper
- Narrow double-sided adhesive basting tape
- ½ yd. (45.7cm) medium-weight fusible interfacing
- 5" (12.7cm) gold cord
- 1½" (3.8cm) gold tassel

DIPLOMA

- 3½" × 4½" (8.9cm × 11.4cm) piece of scrapbook paper
- 12" (30.5cm) ribbon, ⅛" (3mm) wide

This image of *Graduation Day Outfit* shows the back side of the gown.

Graduation Gown

1 Cut four front yokes, two back yokes and two sleeves using pattern pieces. Cut two front gowns 6¼" × 10½" (15.9cm × 26.7cm) long. Cut one back gown 12" × 10½" (30.5cm × 26.7cm) long. Place the armhole cutout patterns at each corner of the back gown, and at the right and left corners of the front gown. Cut these out.

2 With right sides together, sew two front yokes to a back yoke at the shoulders. Press the seam allowances open. Repeat with the remaining pieces for the lining.

3 Place the yokes with right sides together and stitch along the center front and neck edges. Clip the curves and turn to the right side. Press. Baste the armhole edges together (Gown 1).

4 Press the center front edges of the front gowns ½" (13mm) to the wrong side. Make three small pleats on each side of the front gowns. Measure ⅝" (16mm) from the center fold line and make a mark. Measure ¼" (6mm) toward the armhole and make another mark. Fold the fabric toward the folded edge so the second mark meets the first mark. Pin. Repeat the procedure twice more so you have three pleats ⅝" (16mm) apart. Press the pleats only about two-thirds of the way down the front (Gown 2).

5 Stitch each front gown to each front yoke with right sides together. Serge or zigzag stitch the seam allowances and press toward the yokes.

6 Mark the center of the top edge of the back gown. Make marks ¾" (19mm) on each side of the center mark. Fold these marks so they meet at

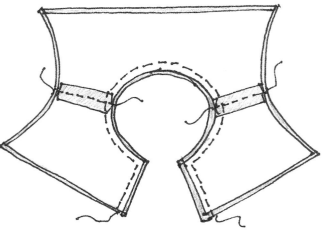

Gown 1

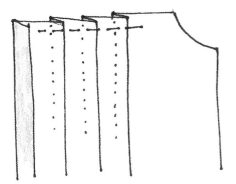

Gown 2

the center and pin. Measure 1" (2.5cm) away from one of the pleats. Make a mark and measure ¾" (19mm) and make another mark. Fold the fabric so the second mark meets the first one and pin. Repeat this step so you have three pleats on one side. Make pleats on the remaining side. Press the pleats about two-thirds of the way down the back (Gown 3).

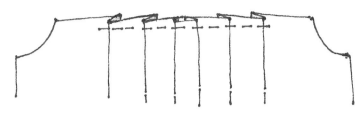

Gown 3

7 Stitch the back gown to the back yoke with right sides together. Serge or zigzag stitch the seam allowance and press toward the yoke.

8 Sew the zipper to the front edges beginning ½" (13mm) from the top edge. Place the left half of the zipper under the pressed edge so the fabric comes to the center of the zipper. Use a piece of the basting tape to hold the zipper to the fabric while stitching. Note that the end of the zipper does not come to the bottom of the gown. Stitch, using a zipper foot. Repeat with the right side of the zipper (Gown 4).

9 Serge or zigzag stitch the lower edge of the sleeves and press ¼" (6mm) to the wrong side. Stitch. Gather the sleeve caps and stitch to the armholes with right sides together.

10 Stitch the side seams from the sleeve edge to the bottom edge of the gown (Gown 5).

11 Serge or zigzag stitch the lower edge of the gown and press ½" (13mm) to the wrong side. Topstitch ¼" (6mm) from the pressed edge.

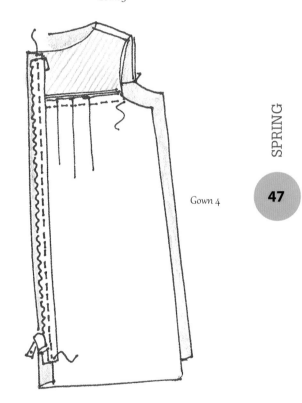

Gown 4

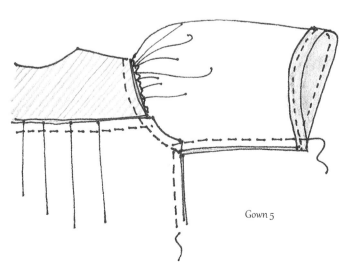

Gown 5

Graduation Cap

1 Cut two cap tops from the fabric and interfacing. (Be sure to cut the hole in only one of the fabric and interfacing tops.) Cut two cap risers from the fabric and one from the interfacing.

2 Fuse the interfacing to the wrong side of one of the fabric risers. Sew the risers together along the curved bottom edge (Cap 1). Clip the curves and turn to the right side and press. Open out the short edges and stitch with right sides together. Press the seam allowances open. Baste the unstitched edges together.

3 Fuse the interfacing to each cap top. With right sides together, stitch the basted edges of the cap riser to the hole in the center of one top. Serge or zigzag stitch the seam allowances and press toward the riser (Cap 2).

4 With right sides together, sew the remaining cap top to the cap with the riser, leaving a small opening on the side (Cap 3). Turn to the right side and press. Topstitch close to the pressed edge.

5 Sew the tassel to one end of the cord. Sew the other end of the cord to the center of the cap (Cap 4).

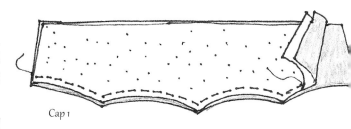

Cap 1

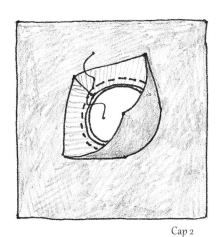

Cap 2

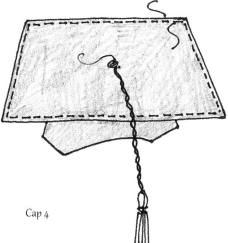

Cap 3

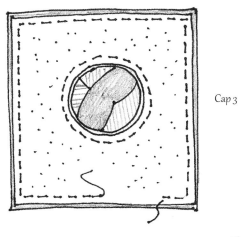

Cap 4

My Doll's Diploma

1 Print a graduation message on the paper. An example would be:

> Certificate of Graduation
> This is to certify that
> (Doll's name)
> has completed second grade.

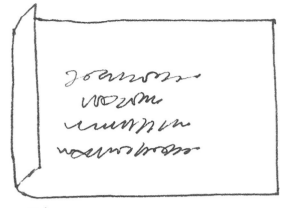

Diploma 1

2 Roll the paper from the 3½" (8.9cm) side into a tube about ½"–⅝" (13mm–16mm) wide (Diploma 1).

3 Tie the ribbon around the tube (Diploma 2).

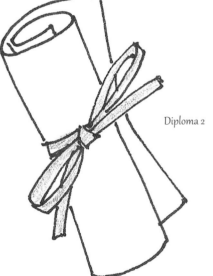

Diploma 2

a project to make together!

Special Occasion Dress

Anna loves donning her new special occasion dress to attend spring theater and dance concerts. She wore it as she watched her local ballet company's production of *Swan Lake* so that she could feel like a princess, too!

See a 360-degree view of this outfit here: www.marthapullen.com/doll-fashion-studio.html

SUPPLIES:

- Patterns No. 41, No. 42, No. 43, No. 44, No. 45
- ½ yd. (45.7cm) satin or other shiny fabric (for dress and lining)
- ¼ yd. (22.9cm) contrasting color satin (for borders)
- 4" (10.2cm) Velcro strip, cut in half

Dress

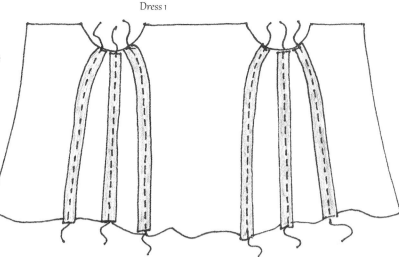

Dress 1

1 Cut one front, two backs and four side panels from the satin fabric. Cut the same pieces out again for the lining. Cut two front borders, four back borders, two 1½" × 8" (3.8cm × 20.3cm) pieces for the bows and two 1½" × 4" (3.8cm × 10.2cm) pieces for the straps from the contrasting fabric.

2 With right sides together, sew a side panel to one side of the dress front. Sew another side panel to the other side of the dress front. Press the seam allowances open.

3 With right sides together, sew a side panel to the side of the left dress back. Sew the other side panel to the side of another dress back. Press the seam allowances open.

4 Sew the side seams of the dress with right sides together. Press the seam allowances open (Dress 1).

5 Repeat steps 2–4 for the lining pieces.

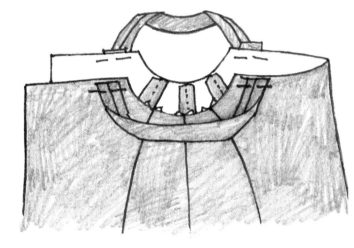

Dress 2

6 Fold the strap pieces in half lengthwise with right sides together and stitch along the long edges. Turn to the right side and press so the seam line is in the middle of the wrong side of the strap. Place one end of each strap on the right side of the top front edge ¼" (6mm) away from the armhole and baste. Place the other end of the strap on the top back edge ½" (13mm) from the armhole. Baste (Dress 2).

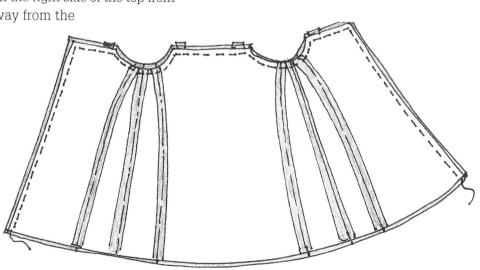

Dress 3

7 Place the dress and the lining right sides together and stitch up one center back, across the top of the right dress back, around the armhole, across the top of the dress front, around the second armhole, across the top of the left dress back and down the remaining center back. Clip the curves; trim the corners and turn to the right side. Press (Dress 3).

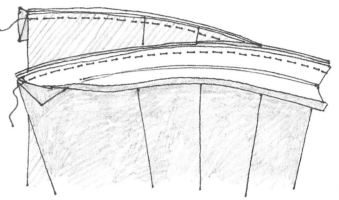

Dress 4

8 Baste the lower edges of the dress and the lining together. From now on, this lower edge will be treated as one.

9 Sew the side edges of the front border to the side edge of each back border. Press the seam allowances open. Repeat with the border lining. Stay stitch along the top edges because these curved edges can stretch.

10 With right sides together, sew the lower edges and center back ends of the border and the border lining (Dress 4). Clip the curves; turn to the right side and press. Press the top edge of the lining ¼" (6mm) to the wrong side. Pin the top edge of the border to the lower edge of the dress with right sides together. Stitch, making sure not to catch the border lining in your stitching (Dress 5). Press the seam allowances toward the border. Pin the pressed edge of the lining over the seam line and slip stitch to secure (Dress 6).

Dress 5

11 Lapping right over left, sew the Velcro strip to the center back opening.

12 Fold the bow pieces in half lengthwise with right sides together and stitch along the long edges and one short end. Turn to the right side and press. Fold the remaining end ¼" (6mm) to the wrong side and hand stitch closed. Tie each one into a bow and hand-tack over the stitching of the straps in the front (Dress 7).

Dress 6

Dress 7

Spring Break Outfit

SUPPLIES:

PANTS, SHIRT, TOP

- Pattern No. 46 (for capri pants)
- Patterns No. 47, No. 48, No. 49 (for T-shirt)
- Patterns No. 50, No. 51 (for sleeveless top)
- ¼ yd. (22.9cm) print fabric (for top and pants cuffs)
- ¼ yd. (22.9cm) contrasting print fabric (for pants)
- 11" (27.9cm) elastic, ¼" (6mm) wide
- 2" (5.1cm) Velcro strip, cut in half (for top)
- ¼ yd. (22.9cm) knit fabric (for T-shirt)
- 1¼" × 8¼" (3.2cm × 21.0cm) piece of knit ribbing*

   * **(If unable to find matching ribbing, cut a 1¼" × 8¼" [3.2cm × 21.0cm] strip from the knit fabric.)**

- 3" (7.6cm) Velcro strip, cut in half, or 3 snaps

SHOULDER PURSE

- Pattern No. 52
- 4" × 7" (10.2cm × 17.8cm) piece of felt
- 3" (7.6cm) trim, ½" (13mm) wide
- Fabric glue or glue stick
- Crewel hand sewing needle, size 7
- 1 skein of coordinating embroidery floss
- 10" (25.4cm) ribbon, ⅜" (10mm) wide
- Matching sewing thread

This stylish ensemble is perfect for Lauren's family vacation to visit her grandparents. Her purse is trimmed with multicolored flowers, making it a perfect accessory for any spring outfit.

See a 360-degree view of this outfit here: www.marthapullen.com/doll-fashion-studio.html

Capri Pants

1 Cut four pants from the contrasting print fabric. Cut two cuffs 2½" × 6½" (6.4cm × 16.5cm) from the print fabric.

2 With right sides together, sew the side seams of two pants and press. Repeat with the remaining pants pieces.

3 Press the cuffs in half lengthwise with wrong sides together. Place the cuffs to the wrong side of each pant leg and stitch. Fold the cuffs to the right side of the pants and press.

4 Stitch the center front seam with right sides together and press (Pants 1).

5 Serge or zigzag stitch the top edge of the pants and press ½" (13mm) to the wrong side. Stitch ⅜" (10mm) from the folded edge to create a casing. Thread the elastic through the casing and secure the ends (Pants 2).

6 Stitch the center back seam with right sides together.

7 Sew the inner leg seam (Pants 3).

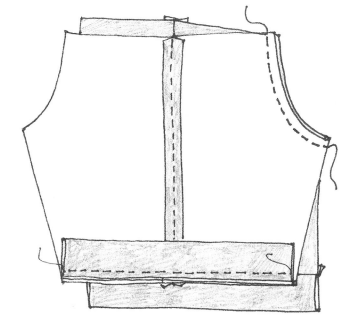

Pants 1

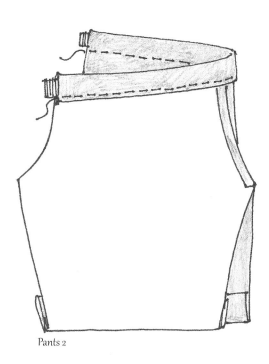

Pants 2

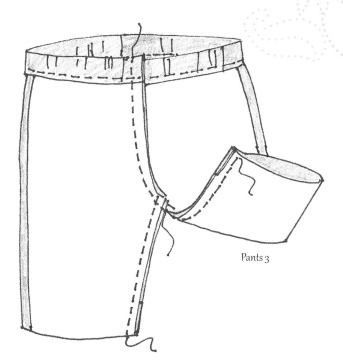

Pants 3

T-Shirt

1 Cut one front, two backs and two sleeves from the knit fabric.

2 With right sides together, sew the backs to the front at the shoulder seams.

3 Press the center back edges ¼" (6mm) to the wrong side and stitch (Shirt 1).

4 Fold the ribbing in half lengthwise with right sides together. Stitch the short ends and turn to the right side. Stretching the ribbing to fit the neckline, stitch both edges of the ribbing to the neckline (Shirt 2).

5 Press the sleeve edges ¼" (6mm) to the wrong side. Stitch close to the cut edge with one or two rows of stitching, or use a double needle.

6 With right sides together, sew the sleeve caps to the armholes, easing as necessary. Stitch the underarm seam from the sleeve edges to the bottom of the shirt.

7 Press the lower edge of the shirt ½" (13mm) to the wrong side and stitch in the same manner as the sleeve edges (Shirt 3).

8 Lapping right over left, sew the Velcro or snaps to the back opening.

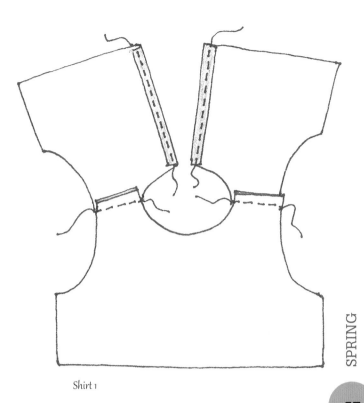

Shirt 1

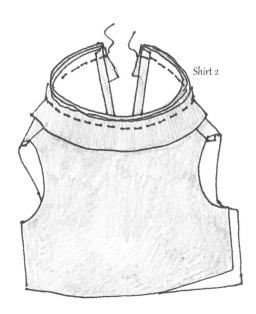

Shirt 2

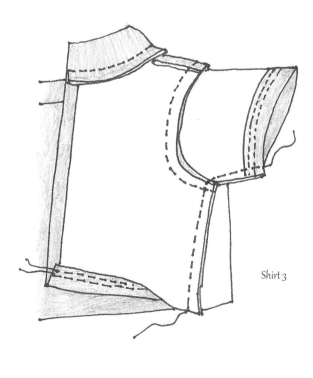

Shirt 3

Sleeveless Top

1 Cut two fronts, four backs and one ruffle 3" × 27" (7.6cm × 68.6cm) from the print fabric.

2 With right sides together, sew the shoulder seams of one front to two of the backs. Press the seam allowances open. Repeat with the remaining pieces for the lining.

3 Sew the lining to the top up each center back, around the neckline and each armhole. Clip the corners and the curves and turn to the right side. Press (Top 1).

4 Sew the side seams and stitch with right sides together.

5 Serge or zigzag stitch the lower edge and each end of the ruffle. Press them ¼" (6mm) to the wrong side and topstitch. Gather the upper edge of the ruffle and stitch to the top with right sides together (Top 2).

6 Lapping right over left, sew the Velcro to the back opening.

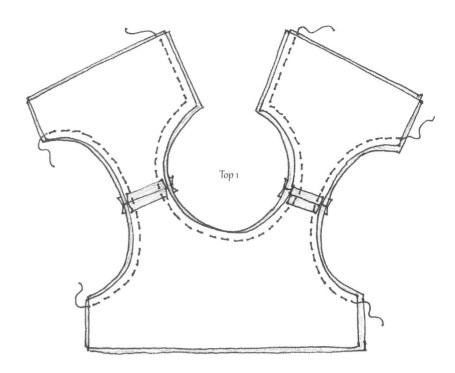

Top 1

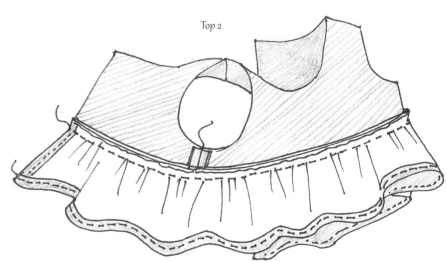

Top 2

My Doll's Shoulder Purse

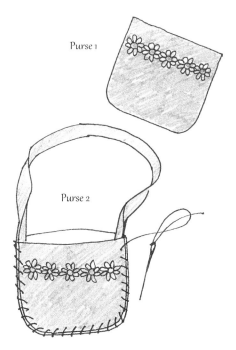

Purse 1

Purse 2

1 Cut two purses from the felt. Glue the trim on the purse front as marked on the pattern piece. If desired, tack the trim with sewing thread to make it more secure (Purse 1).

2 Place the two purses with wrong sides together and pin. Thread the needle with three strands of embroidery floss no more than 18" (45.7cm) long. Beginning at the top left, work overcast or whip stitches along the curved sides and bottom edge of the purse. Knot the thread inside the top right corner with a few stitches made in one place (Purse 2).

3 Pinch the ends of the ribbon and place them inside the top of the purse at the sides and pin. Tack them in place with sewing thread.

a project to make together!

Recital Dress

Katy has a new dress to wear for her spring band concert and choir recital. She's excited to perform the songs she's been practicing for her friends and family. She even has a small solo!

See a 360-degree view of this outfit here: www.marthapullen.com/doll-fashion-studio.html

SUPPLIES:

- Patterns No. 53, No. 54, No. 55, No. 56
- ½ yd. (45.7cm) fabric
- ½ yd. (45.7cm) bias strip of contrasting fabric, 1" (2.5cm) wide
- Paper-backed fusible web, ¼" (6mm) wide strip
- 3" (7.6cm) Velcro strip, cut in half

Dress

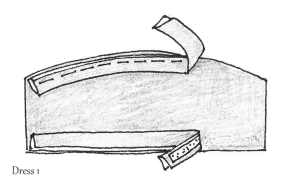

Dress 1

1 Cut one upper front bodice, one lower front bodice, one front bodice lining, four back bodices and one 6" × 36" (15.2cm × 91.4cm) skirt.

2 Fold the bias strip in half lengthwise and press. Cut a piece to fit on the curved edge of the lower bodice and baste. Place a piece of the fusible web on the remaining bias strip and peel away the paper. Fuse the strip to the bottom edge of the lower bodice (Dress 1). Slightly gather the lower edge of the upper bodice. With right sides together, sew the upper and lower bodices. Press the seam so the bias strip is toward the top.

3 With right sides together, sew the front to two backs at the shoulders. Press the seam allowances open and repeat with the remaining pieces for the lining (Dress 2).

4 Stitch the lining to the bodice around the neckline, each center back, and the armholes. Clip the curves and corners, turn to the right side and press (Dress 3).

5 Open out the side seams and stitch (Dress 4).

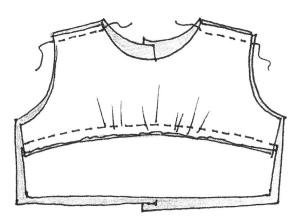

Dress 2

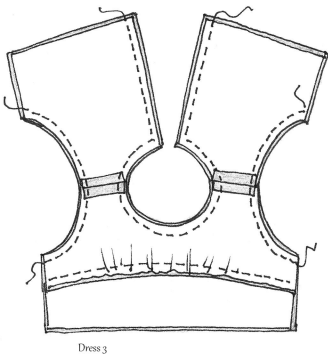

Dress 3

6 Serge or zigzag stitch the sides and one long edge of the skirt. Press the edges ½" (13mm) to the wrong side and stitch.

7 Gather the top edge of the skirt and stitch to the bodice with right sides together (Dress 5).

8 Lapping right over left, sew the Velcro to the back edge.

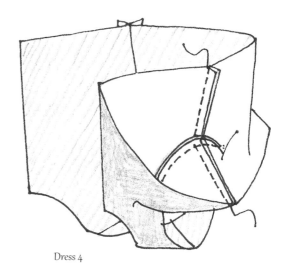

Dress 4

Doll Fashion Tip

The sleeveless style of this dress is very fashionable, but you can also make it with sleeves. Use the pattern pieces and instructions from the *Sweet Valentine's Day Dress* (page 26) or the *Back-to-School Blouse* (page 98). The sleeves should be added before the side seams are sewn.

Dress 5

Rainy Day Fashion Raincoat

Chloe loves to put on her raincoat and splash through puddles after a spring thunderstorm. She enjoys watching the flowers as they begin to bloom into beautiful bouquets.

See a 360-degree view of this outfit here: www.marthapullen.com/doll-fashion-studio.html

SUPPLIES:

- Patterns No. 57, No. 58, No. 59, No. 60
- ½ yd. (45.7cm) laminated cotton or waterproof polyester fabric
- ½ yd. (45.7cm) cotton fabric for lining
- 5 decorative snaps, size 14

Raincoat

1 Cut two fronts, one back, two sleeves and two hoods from the laminated fabric. Cut the same pieces from the lining fabric. Cut one hood ruffle 2½" × 24" (6.4cm × 61.0cm) and two sleeve ruffles 1½" × 10" (3.8cm × 25.4cm) from the lining fabric.

2 With right sides together, sew the back to a sleeve at the shoulder seam. Repeat with the other sleeve to the shoulder seam of the back. Sew the fronts to the other shoulder seam of the sleeves. Finger press the seam allowances open. Repeat with the same lining pieces (Raincoat 1).

3 With right sides together, sew the hoods along the center seam (Raincoat 2). Repeat with the lining. Finger press the center seam allowance. Fold the hood ruffle in half lengthwise with wrong sides together. Gather the cut edges to fit the face edge of the hood. Baste the ruffle to the hood (Raincoat 3). With right sides together, sew the hood to the lining along the face edge (Raincoat 4). Turn to the right side and press on the lining side. Topstitch close to the seam line.

4 Gather the lower edge of the hood (treating the hood and lining as one) to fit the neckline seam between the dots marked on the pattern piece (Raincoat 5). Stitch the hood to the coat with right sides together (Raincoat 6). Trim the seam and clip the curves.

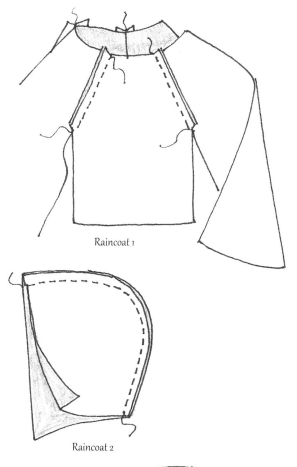

Raincoat 1

Raincoat 2

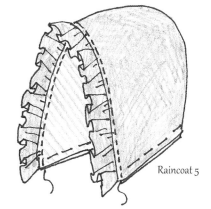

Raincoat 3

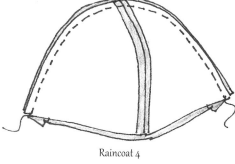

Raincoat 4

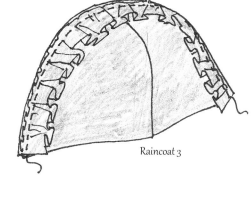

Raincoat 5

5 Fold the sleeve ruffles in half with wrong sides together. Gather the cut edges and stitch to the sleeve edges (Raincoat 7).

6 Sew the lining to the coat with right sides together along the lower front edges, the center fronts, around the neckline (the hood will be inside), the lower sleeve edges and along the lower back edge (Raincoat 8). Clip any curves and turn to right side. Press from the lining side. Topstitch close to the edge along the center fronts, sleeve edges and lower edges. Topstitch just below the hood/coat seam on the coat all the way to the front edges.

7 With right sides together, sew the underarm seams from the sleeve edge to the lower edge of the raincoat. Press from the lining side (Raincoat 9).

8 Apply the five snaps to the front opening of the coat where marked on the pattern piece, following the manufacturer's instructions.

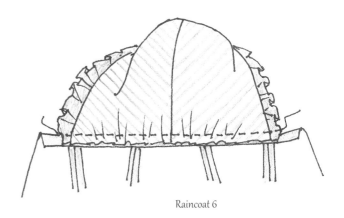

Raincoat 6

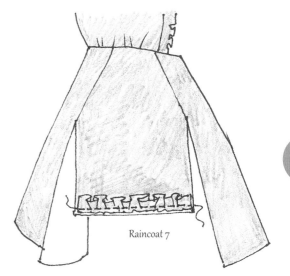

Raincoat 7

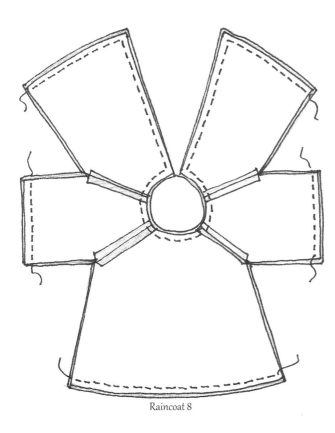

Raincoat 8

Raincoat 9

Chapter 4

Summer Fashion

Summer is a wonderful time for lazy days spent with family and friends. Picnics, eating ice cream before it melts and jumping rope with your best pal are so much fun. Make a doll's fashionable summer wardrobe for this carefree time of year.

Sleepovers in the backyard are much more fun with the *Hot Summer Night PJs* (page 70). Knit fabric is used for both the top and pants, although woven cotton fabric can be used for the top with good success. The top has drawstrings with ribbon ties and a ruffle at the lower edge. The simple pants use lingerie elastic at the waist.

Birthday parties are the highlight of the year for every girl. Her doll wears a pretty polka dot *Birthday Party Dress* (page 76) with a square neckline and cap sleeves. The gathered skirt is attached to the bodice, and a ribbon sash is stitched to the dress.

Make the *Forest Trail Hiking Outfit* (page 82) for playtime or a walk in the woods. The denim shorts have elastic in the back waistline and feature cargo pockets stitched on each side. Use another sturdy cotton fabric if you prefer. The hoodie has a pocket on the front as well as ribbing at the lower edge and sleeves. The back is open all the way into the hood and is closed with Velcro for easy dressing.

The *Sunny Day Sundress* (page 88) features a split bodice in the front and is trimmed with rickrack. The bodice is made in two halves that are overlapped before the gathered skirt is attached.

Idle days call for a day at the spa. This *Spa Day Outfit* (page 92) features a wrap made from stretch terry with gingham bias binding for the edges and straps. The matching cotton fabric eye mask has a medium-weight interfacing to add body.

A *Sleeping Bag and Pillow* (page 74), and a *Birthday Crown* (page 81) are great accessory projects to make together with the doll's owner. The sleeping bag and pillow require machine sewing, so adult help will be needed. The straight stitching makes it a good learning project on a sewing machine. And because every girl wants a crown to wear on her special day, make an easy crown from stiffened felt, sequins and jewels. Girls can easily cut and glue this project, but they may need help with the required stitching.

Hot Summer Night PJs

SUPPLIES:

TOP AND PANTS

- Pattern No. 61 (for top)
- Pattern No. 62 (for pants)
- ¼ yd. (22.9cm) print knit fabric (for top)
- 1 yd. (1m) ribbon, ¼" (6mm) wide
- ¼ yd. (22.9cm) solid knit fabric (for pants)
- 10" (25.4cm) decorative or lingerie elastic, ½" (13mm) wide

PILLOW

- 2 pieces 8½" × 6" (21.6cm × 30.5cm) of flannel or cotton fabric
- Polyester stuffing

SLEEPING BAG

- 20" × 25" (50.8cm × 63.5cm) piece of flannel or cotton fabric (for outside of bag)
- 20" × 25" (50.8cm × 63.5cm) piece of flannel or cotton fabric (for bag lining)
- 20" × 25" (50.8cm × 63.5cm) piece of lightweight batting
- Paper backed fusible web, if desired

See a 360-degree view of this outfit here: www.marthapullen.com/doll-fashion-studio.html

Lauren plans many sleepovers with her friends. In the summer they like to grab sleeping bags and lay out in the backyard to watch flickering fireflies. Sometimes they even see shooting stars!

PJ Top

1 Cut two tops and two ruffles 2" × 27" (5.1cm × 68.6cm) from the print knit fabric.

2 Press the armhole edges on both tops ¼" (6mm) to the wrong side and zigzag stitch. Press the upper edge of both tops ¾" (19mm) to the wrong side and zigzag stitch ½" (13mm) from the pressed edge to make a casing (Top 1).

3 Serge or zigzag stitch the lower edges of the ruffles and press ½" (13mm) to the wrong side. Stitch.

4 Gather the remaining long edges and stitch to the lower edge of each top with right sides together (Top 2).

5 With right sides together, sew the side seams.

6 Cut two pieces of ribbon 15" (38.1cm) long. Thread each piece through the front and back casings (Top 3). Tack the ribbon at the center front and back to prevent the ribbon from being pulled out. Make a bow with the remaining ribbon and tack it to the center front.

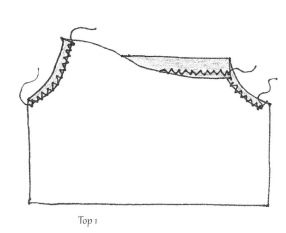

Top 1

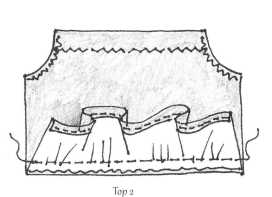

Top 2

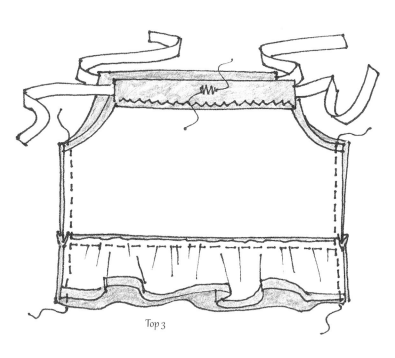

Top 3

PJ Pants

1 Cut two pants from the knit fabric. With right sides together, sew the pants along the center front seam and press (Pants 1).

2 Press the lower leg edges ¼" (6mm) to the wrong side and topstitch.

3 Place one end of the elastic at the center back seam, overlapping the top edge of the leggings. Pull the elastic to the other side while zigzag stitching it in place (Pants 2).

4 Sew the center back seam with right sides together (Pants 3).

5 Sew the inner leg seam (Pants 4).

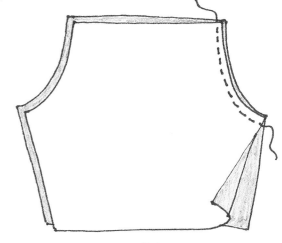

Pants 1

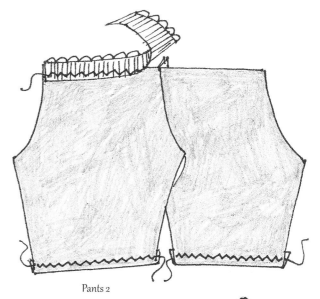

Pants 2

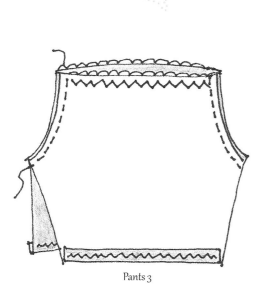

Pants 3

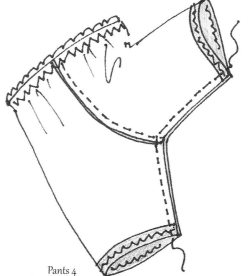

Pants 4

My Doll's
Sleeping Bag and Pillow

projects to make together!

Sleeping Bag

1 Fuse the batting to the wrong side of the top layer of fabric to stabilize the layers before stitching.

2 With right sides together, stitch the lining to the top/batting layer around the edges with a ⅝" (16mm) seam allowance, leaving a 5"– 6" (12.7cm–15.2cm) opening in one side (Bag 1).

3 Trim the batting close to the seam line. Trim the other seam allowances. Turn right side out and press.

4 Topstitch around all edges, making sure to stitch the opening.

5 Fold in half, bringing the short edges together, to form a bag. Topstitch the side and bottom edges together. Begin your stitching on the side about one-third of the way from the top of the bag (Bag 2).

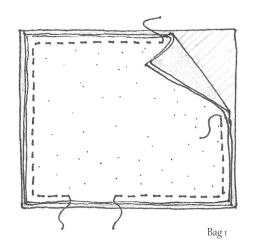

Bag 1

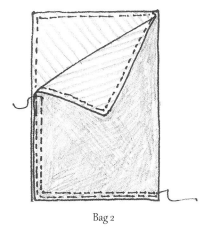

Bag 2

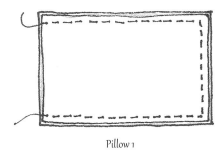

Pillow 1

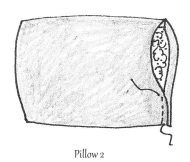

Pillow 2

Pillow

1 With right sides together, stitch along the two 8½" × 6" (21.6cm × 15.2cm) sides and one of the 6" (15.2cm) sides (Pillow 1). Trim the corners, turn to the right side, and press.

2 Lightly fill the pillow with stuffing. Stitch the remaining 6" (15.2cm) side closed (Pillow 2).

Birthday Party Dress

Chloe loves feeling like the Birthday Queen on her special day! She gets to wear a sparkling jeweled crown that she made herself, and her friends will help her celebrate with a deliciously decorated cake.

See a 360-degree view of this outfit here: www.marthapullen.com/doll-fashion-studio.html

SUPPLIES:

DRESS

- Patterns No. 63, No. 64, No. 65, No. 66, No. 67
- ½ yd. (45.7cm) cotton fabric
- ⅔ yd. (61.0cm) ribbon, ⅝" (16mm) wide
- 4" (10.2cm) Velcro strip, cut in half

BIRTHDAY CROWN

- Pattern No. 68
- 1 square of stiffened craft felt
- 1 yd. (1m) sequin trim-by-the-yard
- 6 stick-on flower jewels
- 1 large stick-on crown jewel
- 1½" (3.8cm) elastic, ¼" (6mm) wide
- Fast-drying craft glue

Dress

1 Cut two fronts, four backs, two sleeves, one front skirt, two back skirts and a ruffle 2½" × 55" (6.4cm × 139.7cm) (this will have to be pieced).

2 With right sides together, sew a front to two backs at the shoulder seams and press open. Repeat with the remaining pieces for the lining (Dress 1).

3 The sleeves are cut on the fold with wrong sides together. Press the fold in each sleeve and gather the curved edge (Dress 2). Pull the gathers so each sleeve measures 3½" (8.9cm). Center the gathered edge on each armhole and baste (Dress 3).

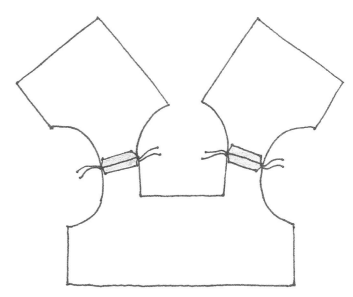

Dress 1

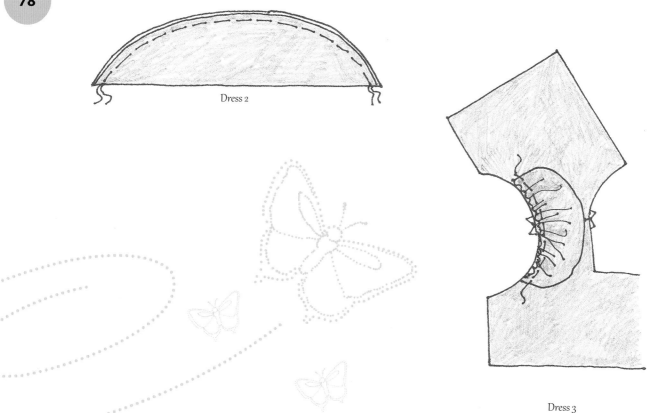

Dress 2

Dress 3

4 Place the lining and dress top right sides together, making sure the sleeves are away from any seam lines. Stitch up one center back, around the neckline and down the other center back. Stitch along the armholes (Dress 4). Clip the curves and corners and turn to the right side. Press. Topstitch along the armhole seam if desired.

5 Stitch the side seams, with right sides together (Dress 5).

6 With right sides together, sew the side seams of the skirt front and backs. Press the center back edges ¼" (6mm) to the wrong side and stitch (Dress 6).

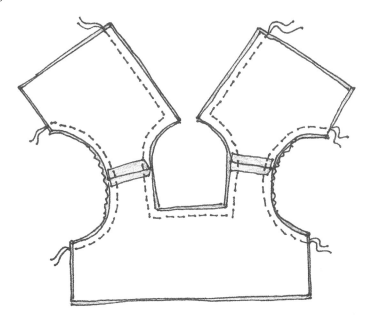

Dress 4

Doll Fashion Tip

Adding a ruffle to the bottom of the dress is easy. Just shorten the skirt by 1" (2.5cm) and cut the ruffle two times the width of the skirt by 1½" (3.8cm). Fold the ruffle in half with wrong sides together and turn the ends to the inside. Gather the top edge and stitch to the skirt.

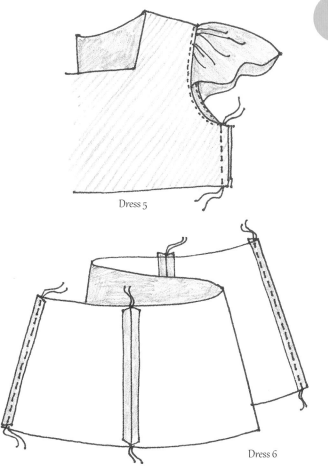

Dress 5

Dress 6

7 Fold the ruffle in half lengthwise with right sides together and stitch each end. Turn to the right side and stitch. Gather the cut edges to fit the bottom of the skirt and stitch with right sides together (Dress 7). Press the gathered edge toward the skirt and topstitch.

8 Gather the top edge of the skirt to fit the dress top and stitch.

9 Fold one end of the ribbon ¼" (6mm) to the wrong side and pin over the center back just below the waistline seam. Stitch along one side with a very narrow zigzag stitch, turning the end under at the other center back edge. Stitch along the other side of the ribbon (Dress 8). Make a bow with the remaining ribbon and tack it to the ribbon at the center front.

10 Lapping right over left, stitch the Velcro to the back opening.

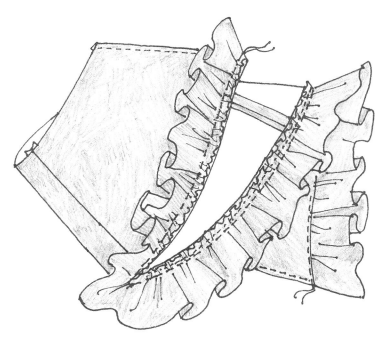

Dress 7

Dress 8

My Doll's Birthday Crown

Crown 1

1 Trace the crown onto the wrong side of the felt and cut it out.

2 Glue the sequin trim to the top and bottom edges of the crown.

3 Place the large crown jewel in the center of the crown and three of the flower jewels along each side (Crown 1). To ensure the jewels will stay permanently, use a dab of glue underneath.

4 With help from your adult helper, fit the crown around the doll's head to see how much elastic you will need. Cut it if necessary. Pin each end of the elastic to the wrong side of the crown and stitch with a wide zigzag stitch.

a project to make together!

Forest Trail Hiking Outfit

Emily seizes every opportunity to take hikes on warm summer days. She likes to watch for wildlife and search for rocks as she and her dog Buddy follow a winding trail through the woods.

See a 360-degree view of this outfit here: www.marthapullen.com/doll-fashion-studio.html

SUPPLIES:

HOODIE AND HIKING SHORTS

- Patterns No. 69, No. 70, No. 71, No. 72, No. 73 (for hoodie)
- Patterns No. 74, No. 75, No. 76 (for shorts)
- ⅓ yd. (30.5cm) sweatshirt fleece fabric
- 3" × 20" (7.6cm × 50.8cm) ribbing
- 8" (20.3cm) Velcro strip, cut in half
- ¼ yd. (22.9cm) lightweight denim
- 4½" (11.4cm) elastic, ¼" (6mm) wide

Hoodie

1 Cut one front, two backs, two sleeves, one pocket and two hoods from the fleece.

2 Pin the curved edges of the pocket ¼" (6mm) to the wrong side and stitch (Hoodie 1). Fold the top and short sides of the pockets to the wrong side and pin to the sweatshirt front as marked on the pattern piece. The bottom edge of the pocket should be flush with the lower edge of the sweatshirt front. Stitch across the top and short sides of the pocket to attach it to the sweatshirt. Baste the bottom edge to the sweatshirt front (Hoodie 2).

3 With right sides together, sew the front to the backs at the shoulder seams and press. Serge the center back edges of the hoodie (Hoodie 3).

4 Serge the curved edge of each hood separately if desired. Stitch the hoods with right sides together from the front edge to the dot marked on the pattern piece and press the seam allowances open. Serge the front edge of the hood and press it ½" (13mm) to the wrong side. Stitch (Hoodie 4).

5 Pin the hood to the neckline so the back edges of the hood are flush with the center backs of the hoodie. Note that the sides of the hood don't meet at the center front. Stitch. Press the seam allowances toward the hoodie and topstitch close to the seam line, including the unstitched area of the neckline (Hoodie 5).

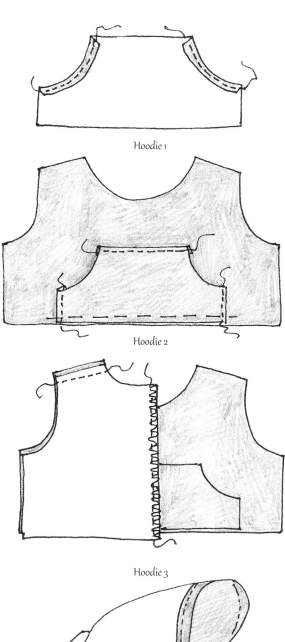

Hoodie 1

Hoodie 2

Hoodie 3

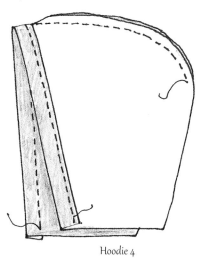

Hoodie 4

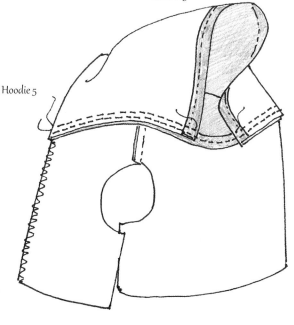

Hoodie 5

6 Cut two pieces of ribbing 1½" × 3½" (3.8cm × 8.9cm). Fold each one in half lengthwise with wrong sides together and stitch to the right side of the lower edge of each sleeve, stretching to fit. Pin the seam allowances to the sleeves and topstitch on the sleeves close to the seam (Hoodie 6). Sew the sleeve caps to the armholes, easing to fit. Sew the underarm seam (Hoodie 7).

7 Cut a piece of ribbing 2½" × 12" (6.4cm × 30.5cm) and fold in half lengthwise with right sides together. Stitch across one end and turn to the right side. Pin the stitched end to the lower edge on the left side of the center back. Pin the unfinished end to the lower edge on the right hand side. Sew the ribbing to the bottom of the hoodie, stretching the ribbing to fit. The right edge will remain unfinished (Hoodie 8).

8 Press the right side of the center back, including the hood, ¼" (6mm) to the wrong side. Sew the hook side of the Velcro under this edge. Sew the loop side to the other center back.

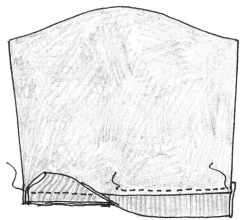

Hoodie 6

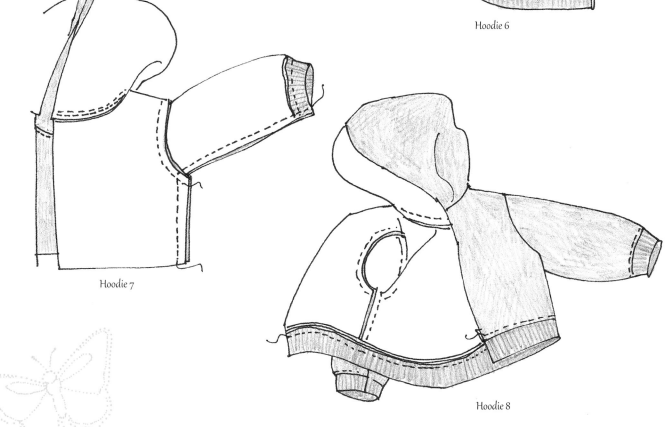

Hoodie 7

Hoodie 8

Hiking Shorts

1 Cut two fronts, two backs, four pockets and a waistband 1½" × 14¼" (3.8cm × 36.2cm).

2 With right sides together, sew the side seams and press (Shorts 1). Press the lower edge ¼" (6mm) to the wrong side. Press another ¼" (6mm) and stitch.

3 Press the short ends of two of the pockets ¼" (6mm) to the wrong side. Sew the pockets together along both long edges and the other short edge (Shorts 2). Clip the corners and turn to the right side. With the open end of the pocket at the bottom, center the pocket on the side seam 1⅛" (2.9cm) from the hem edge. Stitch along the three sides, starting 1" (2.5cm) from the top (Shorts 3). Fold the top of the pocket down 1" (2.5cm) and press. Tack to the pocket. Repeat this step with the remaining two pocket pieces.

4 With right sides together, sew the center front and back seams (Shorts 4).

5 Serge or zigzag stitch along one edge of the waistband. With right sides together, sew the short ends and press the seam allowance open. Sew the unfinished edge of the waistband to the shorts with right sides together, matching the waistband seam to the center back seam of the shorts. Fold the waistband over to the inside of the shorts so the waistband is ½" (13mm) wide. Topstitch in place, leaving a 1" (2.5cm) opening at each side seam for the casing (Shorts 5).

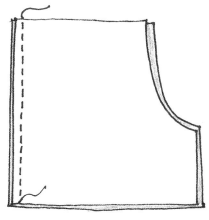

Shorts 1

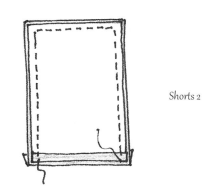

Shorts 2

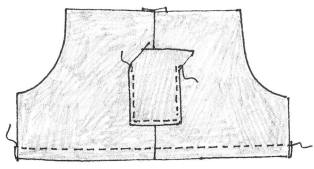

Shorts 3

Shorts 4

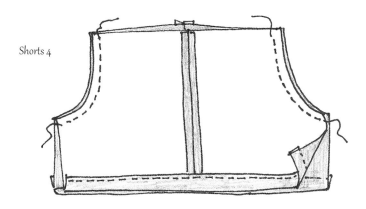

6 Thread the elastic through the back waistband and secure at each side seam. Stitch the openings in the waistband closed.

7 Sew the inner leg seam (Shorts 6).

Shorts 5

Doll Fashion Tip

Adding a snap to the pocket flap on the shorts is simple. Remember to apply the snap before the pocket is stitched to the shorts.

Shorts 6

Sunny Day Sundress

Katy's summery sundress is just right for an afternoon outside with friends. She loves to serve them ice-cold lemonade and cookies under a shady umbrella in the backyard.

See a 360-degree view of this outfit here: www.marthapullen.com/doll-fashion-studio.html

SUPPLIES:

- Patterns No. 77, No. 78
- ⅓ yd. (30.5cm) cotton print fabric
- 1½ yds. (137.2cm) medium rickrack
- 3" (7.6cm) Velcro strip, cut in half

Sundress

1 Cut four fronts, four backs, one skirt 5¾" × 36" (14.6cm ×91.4cm) and a strip 1½" × 7½" (3.8cm × 19.1cm).

2 With right sides together, sew the strip lengthwise. Press the seam allowance open and turn to the right side. Press so the seam allowance is in the center. Cut in half to make two 3¾" (9.5cm) straps (Sundress 1).

3 Baste the rickrack over the curved seam line on two front sections. Baste the rickrack to the top edge of two back sections. With right sides together, sew the backs to the fronts at the side seams. Press the seam allowances open. Sew the remaining fronts and backs for the lining.

4 Pin one end of the strap to the front top edge as ½" (13mm) from the armhole curve. Pin the other end to the back top edge ½"(13mm) from the armhole curve (Sundress 2). Sew one top to the lining by stitching around the curved front edge, armholes, across the top back and down the center back (Sundress 3). Clip the curves and corners. Turn to the right side and press. Repeat with the other half of the top.

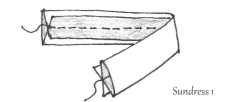

Sundress 1

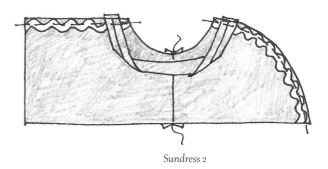

Sundress 2

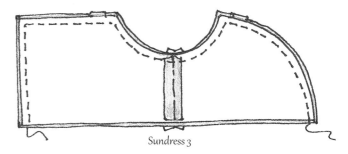

Sundress 3

Sundress 4

5 Place the right half of the top over the left by 1½" (3.8cm). Baste. Tack the right front to the left at the top where they meet (Sundress 4).

6 Serge or zigzag stitch the sides and lower edge of the skirt. Press ¼" (6mm) to the wrong side and stitch. Place the remaining rickrack under the hem edge so the peaks extend below the hem. Turn each end under before stitching (Sundress 5).

7 Gather the top edge of the skirt and stitch to the top with right sides together. Serge or zigzag stitch the seam allowances.

8 Lapping right over left, sew the Velcro to the back opening.

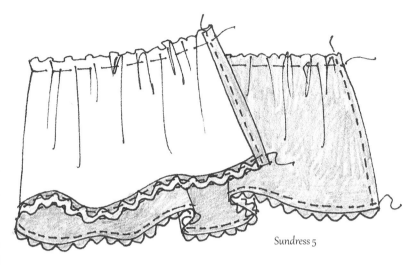

Sundress 5

Doll Fashion Tip

The look of this dress can be altered by using another trim on the bodice and skirt. Once the bodice is stitched, apply a trim such as the flowers shown on the purse on page 59. Place it about ¼" below the top edge and stitch.

Spa Day Outfit

SUPPLIES:

WRAP AND MASK

- Pattern No. 79 (for wrap)
- Pattern No. 80 (for mask)
- ¼ yd. (22.9cm) stretch terry fabric (for wrap)
- 6" (15.2cm) square of matching cotton fabric (for mask)
- 3" × 5" (7.6cm × 12.7cm) piece of fusible interfacing
- 2" × 65" (5.1cm × 165.1cm) bias strip (for wrap)
- 1¼" × 13" (3.2cm × 33.0cm) bias strip (for mask)
- Bias tape makers, sizes 25 and 18
- Purchased ribbon rose, size 1" (2.5cm)
- Purchased bow with ribbon rosette (for mask)
- 2 snaps
- 8" (20.3cm) elastic, ¼" (6mm) wide

See a 360-degree view of this outfit here: www.marthapullen.com/doll-fashion-studio.html

Anna likes to work hard, but she knows that taking time for herself is important, too! A day at the spa is a great way for her to relax and recharge in between spending time with her friends.

Spa Wrap

1 Cut one wrap from the stretch terry.

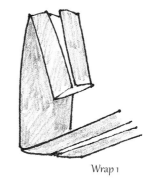

Wrap 1

2 Using the larger bias tape maker, press the 2" (5.1cm) bias strip to make a 1" (2.5cm) bias with folded sides (Wrap 1). Press the bias in half to make a doubled folded strip ½" (13mm) wide.

3 Beginning at the top left corner, place the cut edge of the fabric inside the strip and stitch, mitering the corners. Continue around the armholes, across the front top edge, down the side, across the bottom edge and back up to the point where you began. Cut the tape and turn the end under as you finish the stitching (Wrap 2).

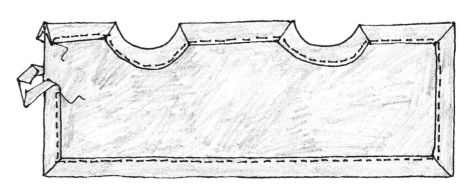

Wrap 2

4 Cut two straps 5" (12.7cm) long from the bias. Turn the ends ¼" (6mm) to the wrong side and stitch the straps closed. Place each end of the straps under the top edge as marked on the pattern piece and stitch.

5 Sew the snaps to the top edge as marked on the pattern piece. The right side overlaps the left. Tack the large flower to the front corner just below the bias strip (Wrap 3).

Wrap 3

Eye Mask

1 Fuse the interfacing to one side of the fabric. Cut one mask from the fused fabric and another from the other side of the fabric square.

2 Pin the two masks with wrong sides together. Pin the ends of the elastic to the back of the mask at the sides. Baste the ends in place.

3 Make a ⅜" (10mm) bias strip as you did in step 2 of the spa wrap with the smaller bias tape maker. Place the lower edge of the mask inside the folded bias strip and begin stitching around the mask, covering the ends of elastic. Cut the tape and turn the end under as you finish the stitching (Mask).

4 Tack a bow with rosette to the upper right corner if desired.

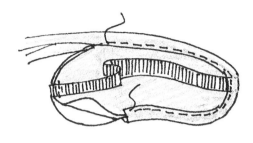

Mask

Doll Fashion Tip

To make this outfit easier, use ready-made double-fold bias tape instead of making your own. It comes in a variety of colors that can be used to match or contrast your fabric.

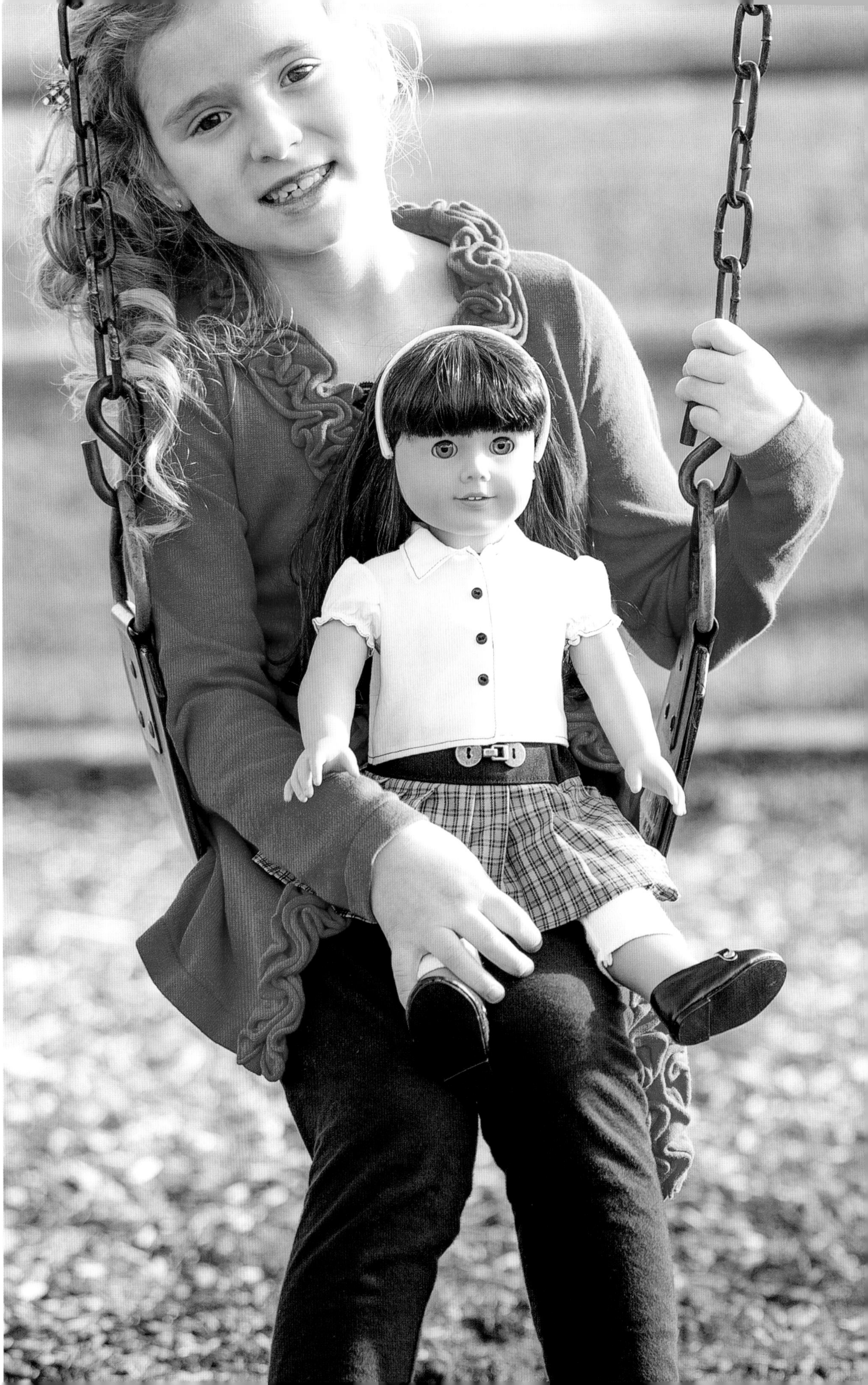

Chapter 5

Fall Fashion

The crunching of leaves under your feet signals the start of cooler fall weather. It is the time for a new school year, cheering on your favorite team, Halloween costumes and family gatherings with fresh baked cookies. All of these occasions call for a new outfit, of course!

For school days, the *Back-to-School Outfit* (page 98) fills the bill. The crisp blouse has a collar, gathered puffed sleeves and buttons down the front. The buttons are sewn over snaps, so buttonholes are not needed.

Cheerleading has always been a fun way for girls to show their team spirit. The *Cheerleader Uniform* (page 104) is made of two pieces. A top is made from a solid color with a white overlay on one side. Contrasting color ribbon is fused on where shown in the photo. The skirt features three knife pleats on the doll's left side. White socks and tennis shoes complete the look.

A casual outfit that can be worn for school is the *Turtleneck T-Shirt Dress* (page 110). It is made from a French terry knit fabric and ribbing for the collar and cuffs. After the skirt is attached, a small pleat is folded over and stitched along the seam line. Add doll suede boots for a very contemporary look.

Any doll will be ready for a baking challenge when she dons her *Baking Day Accessories* (page 114). The apron is lined with the fabric used for the pocket. The neck band is a length of ribbon with a snap at the ends to hold it securely around the doll's neck. The mitt is constructed like other mittens, except the top of the mitt features bias tape and not ribbing.

Halloween is a special time for make-believe. Choosing a special costume each year is a fun challenge. This year's costume is a *Fairy Princess* (page 118). It has a sleeveless square bodice made of satin and trimmed with sequins down the front. The highlight of the outfit is the variegated mesh overskirt, made by gathering a long length of mesh.

Accessory projects to make together with the doll's owner are a *Halloween Mask and Treat Bag* (page 122) for the *Fairy Princess* costume and *Pom-Poms* (page 108) for the cheerleader. Most girls can make the basic mask pieces, but they may need help cutting out the eyes and securing the elastic. Simple pom-poms are made from lengths of foil shred found in the party store and double-sided tape. Some supervision will be needed with these crafts.

Back-to-School Outfit

Lauren knows that you never get a second chance to make a first impression, so she carefully picked out the perfect skirt and blouse for the first day of school. Her confidence and sense of style are sure to turn heads!

See a 360-degree view of this outfit here: www.marthapullen.com/doll-fashion-studio.html

SUPPLIES:

BLOUSE AND SKIRT

- Patterns No. 81, No. 82, No. 83, No. 19 (for blouse)
- Patterns No. 84, No. 85 (for skirt)
- ¼ yd. (22.9cm) cotton fabric (for blouse)
- 3 buttons, size ¼" (6mm)
- 3 snaps
- Topstitching thread
- 8" (20.3cm) elastic, ⅛" (3.1mm) wide
- ¼ yd. (22.9cm) solid color cotton fabric (for skirt)
- ¼ yd. (22.9cm) plaid cotton fabric (for skirt)
- 5" (12.7cm) elastic, ¼" (6mm) wide
- 1 decorative buckle, ⅝" × 1½" (16mm × 3.8cm)

Blouse

1 Cut four fronts, two backs, two sleeves and one collar from the blouse fabric.

2 With right sides together, stitch two fronts to one back at the shoulder seams. Repeat with the other set for the lining. Press the seam allowances open (Blouse 1).

3 Fold the collar in half lengthwise with right sides together. Stitch across the short ends. Clip the corners, turn right side out and press. Topstitch close to the sides and the folded edge with the contrasting thread.

4 With right sides together, center the collar along the neckline of the shirt. The collar does not go all the way to the center front edges. Stitch (Blouse 2).

5 With right sides together, pin the lining to the shirt, sandwiching the collar in between. Sew around the neckline, down the center fronts, and around the hemline in both front and back (Blouse 3). Clip the curves, turn right side out and press. Topstitch close to the center front and lower edges with the contrasting thread. Baste the lining to the shirt around the armholes if desired.

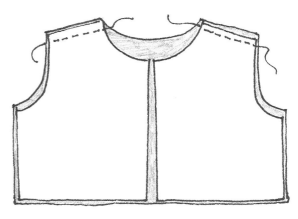

Blouse 1

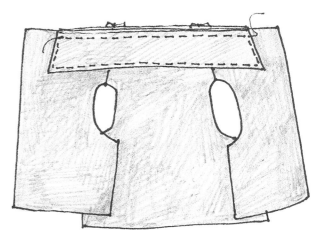

Blouse 2

Blouse 3

6 Serge or zigzag stitch the lower edges of the sleeves and press ¼" (6mm) to the wrong side. Topstitch with the contrasting thread close to the edge. Cut the 8" (20.3cm) elastic in half. Stitch each piece to the lower sleeve edges ¼" (6mm) from the edge. Begin at one side with a few straight stitches. Switch to a wide zigzag stitch and pull the elastic to the other side as you stitch. Secure the end with straight stitches (Blouse 4).

7 Gather the sleeve caps and stitch to the armhole with right sides together. Sew the underarm seam from the sleeve edge to the hem of the blouse (Blouse 5).

8 Sew the buttons on top of the right center front as marked on the pattern piece. Sew the snaps to the right center front as marked on the pattern piece, sewing them underneath each button.

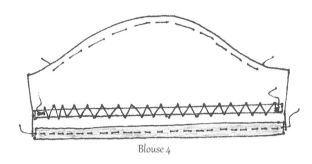

Blouse 4

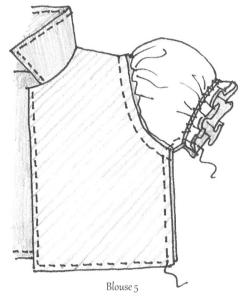

Blouse 5

Skirt

1 Cut two upper skirt fronts and two upper skirt backs. Cut a front lower skirt 4½" × 14¼" (11.4cm × 36.2cm) and a back lower skirt 4½" × 20¾" (11.4cm × 52.7cm).

2 With right sides together, sew the upper fronts along the top edge (Skirt 1). Repeat with the upper backs. Turn to the right side and press. On the upper back skirt, stitch ½" (13mm) away from the top seam line to make a casing (Skirt 2). Set the upper skirts aside.

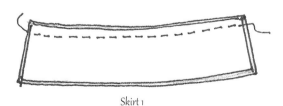

Skirt 1

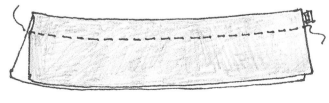

Skirt 2

3 Serge or zigzag stitch the lower edges of the lower skirts and press ¼" (6mm) to the wrong side. Stitch. Begin making knife pleats. Begin 1⅞" (4.8cm) from the right front edge. Make a mark ½" (13mm) away to the right and fold the 1⅞" (4.8cm) mark to meet it. Place a pin in the top edge. Continue making pleats along the top of the skirt, adjusting them as necessary to fit the lower edge of the upper front skirt. Baste the pleats at the top edge and press them in place. Repeat with the lower back skirt (Skirt 3).

4 Thread the 5" (12.7cm) elastic through the back casing and secure the ends.

5 With right sides together, sew the upper front to the lower front. Repeat with the back skirts. Sew the side seams (Skirt 4).

6 Sew the buckle to the upper front about ¾" (1.9cm) from the right seam line as shown (Skirt 5).

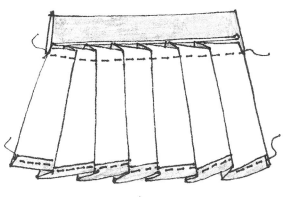

Skirt 3

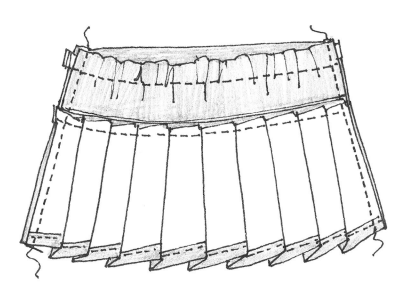

Skirt 4

Skirt 5

Doll Fashion Tip

Pleats are a tradition in school wardrobes. If you want to change from the pleated skirt, simply gather the top edge of the plaid fabric and stitch to the upper skirt. Make this skirt design in several different prints for an easy back-to-school wardrobe.

Cheerleader Uniform

Chloe is ready to showcase her school spirit in her cheerleading outfit. She and her friends love to pump up the crowd before a big game and perform in competitions, especially when she gets to use her sparkly pom-poms!

See a 360-degree view of this outfit here: www.marthapullen.com/doll-fashion-studio.html

SUPPLIES:

TOP AND SKIRT

- Patterns No. 86, No. 87, No. 88 (for top)
- Patterns No. 89, No. 90 (for skirt)
- ⅓ yd. (30.5cm) colored cotton fabric (for skirt and top)
- 5" × 7" (12.7cm × 17.8cm) scrap of white cotton (for top)
- 1 yd. (1m) contrasting color ribbon, ⅜" (10mm) wide
- Paper-backed fusible web, ¼" (6mm) wide strip
- 2½" (6.4cm) Velcro strip, cut in half
- 4½" (11.4cm) elastic, ¼" (6mm) wide

POM-POMS

- 10" (25.4cm) of tiny elastic cord
- 2 wooden candle cups or flower pots with a hole in the bottom, size 1" (2.5cm)
- Double-sided tape
- Foil shreds in desired color (found in gift wrap department)
- Quick-drying craft glue

Top

1 Cut two fronts and four backs from the colored fabric. Cut one angled top from the white fabric.

2 Place the white fabric top over one of the fronts, matching the neckline and shoulders. Cut a strip of ribbon and fusible web to fit the line drawn on the lower left of the front pattern piece. Place the wrong side of the ribbon to the strip, and peel away the paper and fuse it to the top. Cut a strip of ribbon and fusible web long enough to cover the lower raw edge of the white top. Place it on the raw edge and fuse. With matching thread, stitch along each side of the ribbons to secure (Top 1).

3 With right sides together, sew the shoulder seams of the decorated top and two backs. Press the seam allowances open. Repeat with the remaining pieces for the lining (Top 2).

4 Sew the top to the lining with right sides together around the neckline, each center back, lower edges and the armholes. Clip the corners, curves and angles. Turn to the right side through the side seams and press (Top 3).

5 Sew the side seams with right sides together (Top 4).

6 Lapping right over left, sew the Velcro to the back opening.

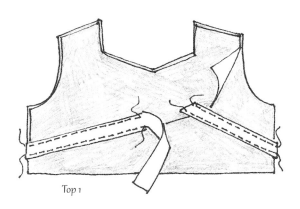

Top 1

Top 2

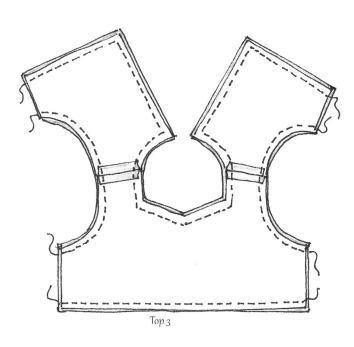

Top 3

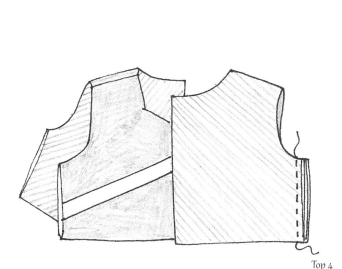

Top 4

Skirt

1 Cut one front, one back and a waistband 1½" × 15" (3.8cm × 38.1cm).

2 Make the three pleats on the left side of the skirt. Following the marks on the pattern piece, fold the fabric to the left so the marked points meet. Pin at the top and baste (Skirt 1). Press the pleats to the bottom of the skirt.

3 With right sides together, sew the side seams.

4 Serge or zigzag stitch the lower edge of the skirt and press ¼" (6mm) to the wrong side (Skirt 2). Stitch. Place the remaining ribbon on the right side of the skirt over the hem using a fusible web strip and fuse. Turn the ends under at the side seam where they meet. Stitch along each side of the ribbon using matching thread. Re-press the pleats.

5 Serge or zigzag stitch along one edge of the waistband. With right sides together, sew the short ends and press the seam allowances open. Sew the unfinished edge of the waistband to the skirt with right sides together, matching the waistband seam to a side seam of the skirt. Fold the waistband over to the inside of the skirt so the waistband is ½" (13mm) wide. Topstitch in place, leaving a 1" (2.5cm) opening at each side seam for the casing (Skirt 3).

6 Thread the elastic through the back waistband and secure at each side seam. Stitch the openings in the waistband closed.

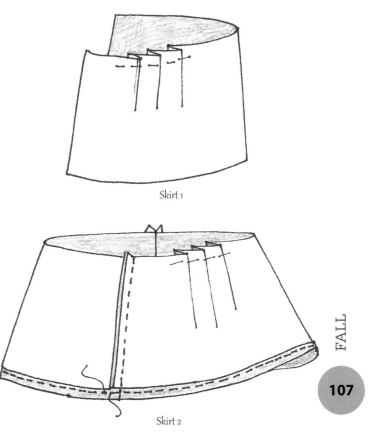

Skirt 1

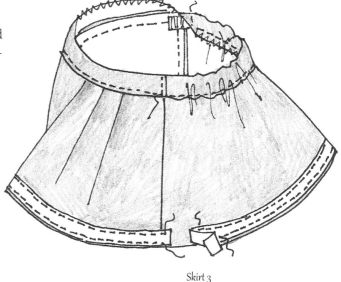

Skirt 2

Skirt 3

My Doll's Cheerleader Pom-Poms

projects to make together!

Cheerleader Pom-Poms

1 Cut the elastic cord to make two 5" (12.7cm) lengths. Fold each in half and knot the cut ends. Thread the loop of the cord through the hole in the wooden cup; use a needle and thread if necessary (Pom-Pom 1). This makes the loop that will fit around the doll's hand.

2 Place 15" (38.1cm) of the double-sided tape on a flat surface and secure it to the surface. Starting at one end, lay the shredded foil one strand at a time even with the top of the tape. Continue along the tape, stopping 2" (5.1cm) before the end.

3 Starting at the same end as before, roll the tape onto itself for the entire length. The last two inches of tape will help secure the strands (Pom-Pom 2).

4 Place the tape inside the cup. Adjust as necessary—trim the tape so it doesn't show, or add more tape to have the end fit snugly in the cup.

5 Remove the roll of strands and apply craft glue to the inside of the cup. Replace the roll of strands and let dry thoroughly (Pom-Pom 3).

6 Trim the ends to approximately 4½"–5" (11.4cm–12.7cm) long. Crunch the strands in your hand to make them crinkled.

7 Repeat with the remaining wooden cup/pot to make a second pompom.

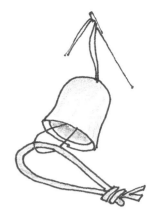

Pom-Pom 1

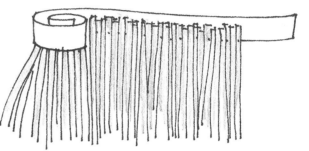

Pom-Pom 2

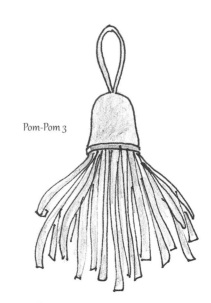

Pom-Pom 3

Turtleneck T-Shirt Dress

Emily likes to stay casual and comfy during the autumn months. Her favorite fall outfit is her turtleneck T-shirt dress that keeps her warm when she walks home from school and plays hopscotch with her friends.

See a 360-degree view of this outfit here: www.marthapullen.com/doll-fashion-studio.html

SUPPLIES:

- Patterns No. 91, No. 92, No. 93
- ¼ yd. (22.9cm) French terry or other knit fabric
- ½ yd. (45.7cm) matching ribbing, 2½" (6.4cm) wide
- 2" (5.1cm) Velcro strip, cut in half

Dress

1 Cut one front, two backs, two sleeves and one skirt 4½" × 18" (11.4cm × 45.7cm) from the knit fabric. Cut one neckband 2½" × 8" (6.4cm × 20.3cm) and two cuffs 2" × 4½" (5.1cm × 11.4cm) from the ribbing.

2 With right sides together, sew the backs to the front at the shoulder seams.

3 Sew the center back seam to 4" (10.2cm) from the neckline. Press the seam allowances open, including the unstitched part of the seam, and topstitch the opening (Dress 1).

4 Fold the neck ribbing in half lengthwise with right sides together. Stitch the short ends and turn to the right side. Stretching the ribbing to fit the neckline, stitch the ribbing through all layers to the right side of the neckline (Dress 2).

5 Fold the cuffs in half lengthwise with wrong sides together. Stitch to the right side of the lower edges of the sleeves through all layers, stretching to fit (Dress 3).

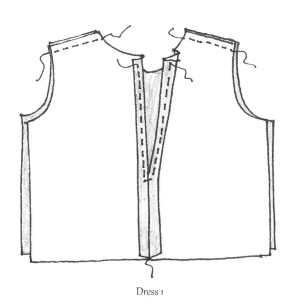

Dress 1

Dress 2

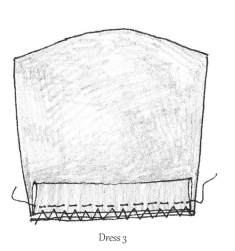

Dress 3

6 With right sides together, sew the sleeve caps to the armholes, easing to fit. Sew the underarm seam from the cuff to the lower edge (Dress 4).

7 Sew the center back edges of the skirt with right sides together. Serge or zig zag stitch the lower edge of the skirt. Press this edge ½" (13mm) to the wrong side and topstitch.

8 Gather the top edge of the skirt slightly and, with right sides together, stitch to the lower edge of the top. Fold the top edge ½" (13mm) over the seam line and stitch the fold to the seam allowance. The stitching will be approximately ½" (13mm) above the fold (Dress 5).

9 Lapping right over left, sew the Velcro to the back opening.

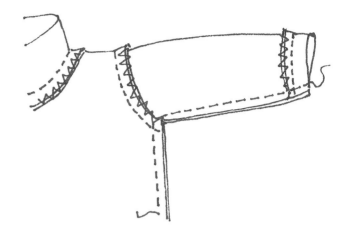

Dress 4

Dress 5

Baking Day Accessories

Katy likes to roll up her sleeves
and bake delicious desserts
on chilly days while wearing
her apron and mitt. She loves
the taste of chocolate and
cinnamon, especially in cookies
and cakes.

See a 360-degree
view of this outfit here:
www.marthapullen.com/doll-
fashion-studio.html

SUPPLIES:

APRON AND MITT
- Patterns No. 94, No. 95 (for apron)
- Pattern No. 96 (for mitt)
- ¼ yd. (22.9cm) print fabric
- ¼ yd. (22.9cm) contrasting print fabric (for lining and pocket)
- Paper-backed fusible web, ¼" (6mm) wide strip
- 1 yd. (1m) ribbon, ⅜" (10mm) wide
- ⅓ yd. (30.5cm) ribbon, ¼" (6mm) wide
- 1 snap
- Seam sealant
- 5" (12.7cm) bias tape

Apron

1 Cut one apron from the print fabric. Cut one apron and one pocket from the contrasting print fabric.

2 Cut 3" (7.6cm) of the ¼" (6mm) ribbon for the pocket. Place the fusible web under the ribbon and peel off the paper. Fuse the ribbon to the pocket ⅜" (10mm) below the fold line on one side. Stitch in place if desired (Apron 1).

3 Fold the pocket on the fold line with right sides together. Stitch around the edge, leaving an opening in the bottom of the pocket for turning (Apron 2). Clip the curves and turn to the right side. Place the pocket on the left side of the apron as marked on the pattern piece. Stitch around the pocket close to the edge.

4 Cut a 4" (10.2cm) piece of ⅜" (10mm) ribbon and fuse it to the top of the apron as in step 3. The ribbon should be placed ¾" (1.9cm) below the top edge. Stitch in place if desired.

5 Cut two 5" (12.7cm) pieces of ⅜" (10mm) wide ribbon for the neck straps. Place one end of each piece on the top of the apron ⅜" (10mm) from the sides of the apron. Baste. Cut two 9" (22.9cm) pieces of ⅜" (10mm) wide ribbon. Place one end of each piece ½" (13mm) below the curved edges on each side. Baste (Apron 3).

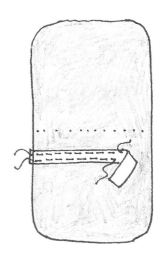

Apron 1

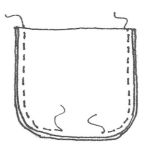

Apron 2

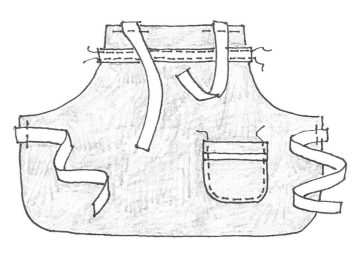

Apron 3

6 With right sides together, sew the apron to the lining around the edges, leaving an opening in the lower edge (Apron 4). Clip the curves and corners and turn to the right side. Press, folding the opening to the inside. Stitch the opening closed.

7 With each size of the remaining ribbon, make bows. Tack the narrow one to the center of the ribbon on the pocket and the larger one to the center of the ribbon of the apron (Apron 5).

8 Fold the ends of the neck straps ½" (13mm) to the wrong side and press. Sew each half of the snap at the ends. Use seam sealant to the ends of the waistline straps to prevent raveling.

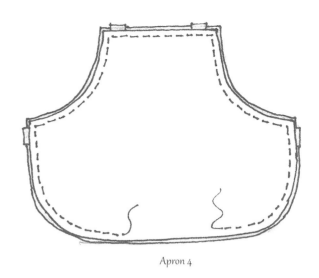

Apron 4

Apron 5

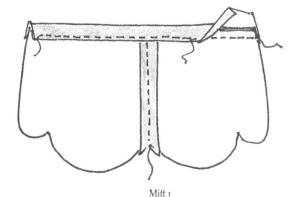

Mitt 1

Mitt 2

Pot Holder Mitt

1 Cut two mitts from the contrasting print fabric.

2 With right sides together, stitch the mitts together up to the dot marked on the pattern piece. Open out flat and press the seam allowances open.

3 Enclose the straight edge on the bottom of the mitt in the bias tape and stitch (Mitt 1).

4 Fold the mitt with right sides together and finish stitching the seam from the dot to the thumb end. Clip the curves, turn to the right side and press (Mitt 2).

Fairy Princess HalloweenCostume

SUPPLIES:

DRESS

- Patterns No. 97, No. 98, No. 99
- ½ yd. (45.7cm) satin
- ½ yd. (45.7cm) fine netting
- 1⅓ yds. (121.9cm) sequin trim, ½" (13mm) wide
- 3" (7.6cm) Velcro strip, cut in half

MASK

- Pattern No. 100
- 3" × 6" (7.6cm × 15.2cm) piece of satin (leftover from dress)
- 3" × 6" (7.6cm × 15.2cm) piece of medium-weight fusible interfacing
- 3" × 6" (7.6cm × 15.2cm) piece of felt
- 8" (20.3cm) elastic, ¼" (6mm) wide
- 12" (30.5cm) sequin trim, ⅛" (3mm) wide
- Fabric glue or glue stick

TREAT BAG

- 4" × 8" (10.2m × 20.3cm) print cotton fabric
- 8" (20.3cm) ribbon, ¼" (6mm) wide

Anna's favorite holiday is Halloween! This year she will dress up as a fairy princess, just like in her storybooks. After trick or treating, she likes to share her candy with her friends (and hide it from her little sister!).

See a 360-degree view of this outfit here: www.marthapullen.com/doll-fashion-studio.html

Dress

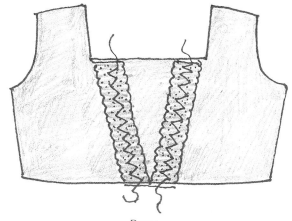

1 Cut two fronts, four backs, one skirt 8½" × 36" (21.6cm × 91.4cm) and two peplums from the satin. Cut the netting skirt 8" × 90" (20.3cm × 228.6cm). (The netting I used was 60" (152.4cm) wide, so I sewed one 60" (152.4cm) length and a 30" (76.2cm) length together. Make sure the seam line won't be in the middle.)

2 Cut two 4" (10.2cm) pieces of trim. Place them on one front on the lines marked on the pattern piece and stitch with a zigzag stitch (Dress 1). With right sides together, sew the shoulders of this front to two backs. Press the seam allowances open. Repeat with the remaining pieces for the lining.

3 With right sides together, sew the lining to the bodice up the center backs, around the neckline and around the armholes (Dress 2). Clip the corners and curves, turn to the right side and press. Open out the sides and stitch with right sides together (Dress 3).

4 Serge or zigzag stitch around the curved edges of each peplum. Press the edges ½" (13mm) to the wrong side. Place the trim over the pressed edge and zigzag stitch (Dress 4). Gather the straight edges and baste them to the bodice with right sides together so the trim meets in the center (Dress 5).

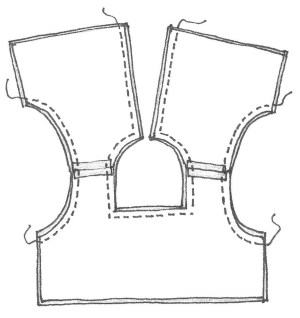

Dress 1

Dress 2

Dress 3

5 Serge or zigzag stitch the sides and one long edge of the satin skirt. Press the edges ½" (13mm) to the wrong side and topstitch. Gather the skirt to fit the bodice (Dress 6). If desired, turn the sides of the net skirt ¼" (6mm) to the wrong side, press another ¼" (6mm) and stitch. Gather one long edge of the net skirt and place it over the gathered satin skirt. Baste together if desired.

6 Sew the skirts to the bodice with right sides together (Dress 7).

7 Lapping right over left, sew the Velcro to the back opening.

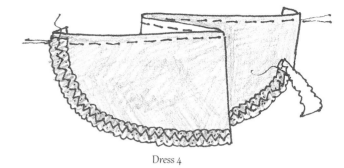

Dress 4

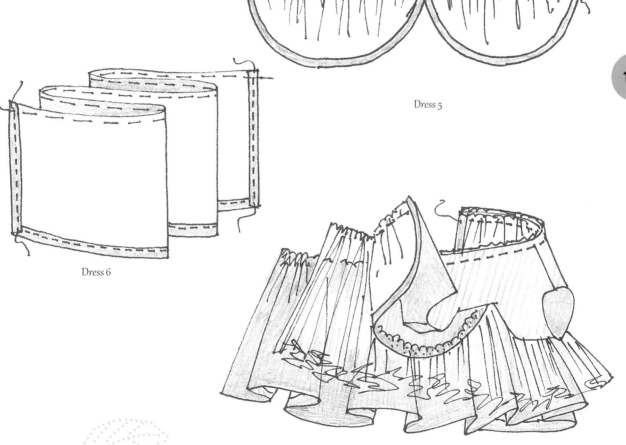

Dress 5

Dress 6

Dress 7

My Doll's Halloween Mask and Treat Bag

projects to make together!

Halloween Mask

1 Fuse the interfacing to the back of the satin. Trace the mask on the interfacing and cut it out. Trace the mask on the felt and cut it out.

2 Glue the felt to the back of the mask, placing the ends of the elastic between the two layers. To secure the elastic, stitch close to the edge of the mask. This stitching will be covered by the trim.

3 Glue the trim around the outside of the mask (Mask).

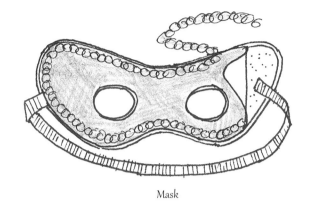

Mask

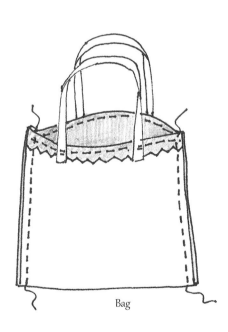

Bag

Treat Bag

1 Serge or zigzag stitch the 4" (10.2cm) ends of the fabric, or cut with a pinking shears. Press this edge ¼" (6mm) to the wrong side and stitch.

2 Cut the ribbon in half for the handles. Stitch the end of each handle ¾" (19mm) from the center of the hemmed edges.

3 With right sides together, fold the rectangle in half to make a rectangle 4" × 3½" (10.2cm × 8.9cm). Stitch the sides together. Turn to the right side and press (Bag).

About the Author

As the owner of Fancywork and Fashion, Joan has written fifteen books of doll clothing patterns, as well as two books with machine embroidery and international embellishment ideas. Her previous book, *All Dolled Up*, features clothes and accessory patterns for girls and their 18" dolls. She publishes a quarterly newsletter for those who love to sew for dolls.

In the fall of 2011, Joan appeared in a two-part series called "30-Minute Doll Clothes" on *Sewing with Nancy*, featuring doll clothing that can be sewn in 30 minutes or less. Her work has been featured in *Sew News*, *Designs in Machine Embroidery* and *Creative Machine Embroidery* magazines. Joan and her husband reside in Minnesota and love to visit their new grandson in New York.

Index

Dedication

Doll Fashion Studio is dedicated to all the young doll owners who will continue the tradition of sewing and crafts with their creativity, boundless energy, and imagination.

Acknowledgements

I wish to express a sincere thank you to several people who helped me with this book.

First, to my talented illustrator Kathy Marsaa for her clear, concise illustrations and several clothing designs.

To two creative doll lovers, Shirley Riley for her sleeping bag design and Connie Blaine for her cheerleader pompoms.

To the staff of F+W Media, especially my editor Kelly Biscopink, for their assistance with my vision for this book.

Lastly, to my favorite proofreader and traveling companion, my husband, Fletcher.

www.fwmedia.com

16 15 14 5 4

DISTRIBUTED IN CANADA BY FRASER DIRECT
100 Armstrong Avenue
Georgetown, ON, Canada L7G 5S4
Tel: (905) 877-4411

DISTRIBUTED IN THE U.K. AND EUROPE BY F&W MEDIA INTERNATIONAL
Brunel House, Newton Abbot, Devon, TQ12 4PU, England
Tel: (+44) 1626 323200, Fax: (+44) 1626 323319
Email: enquiries@fwmedia.com

DISTRIBUTED IN AUSTRALIA BY CAPRICORN LINK
P.O. Box 704, S. Windsor NSW, 2756 Australia
Tel: (02) 4577-3555

SRN: V6715
ISBN-13: 978-1-4402-3091-2

Edited by Kelly Biscopink
Designed by Lisa Fordham
Production coordinated by Greg Nock
Photography by Corrie Schaffeld of 1326 Studios
Photo styling by Kelly O'Dell

Metric Conversion Chart

To convert to	multiply by	
Inches	Centimeters	2.54
Centimeters	Inches	0.4
Feet	Centimeters	30.5
Centimeters	Feet	0.03
Yards	Meters	0.9
Meters	Yards	1.1

Keep Stitching With Us!

Find everything you need—from craft supplies to inspiring books—here at STORE.MARTHAPULLEN.COM

Join the online crafting community!

 Visit us on Facebook:
www.facebook.com/fwcraft

Join us on Twitter:  **@fwcraft**

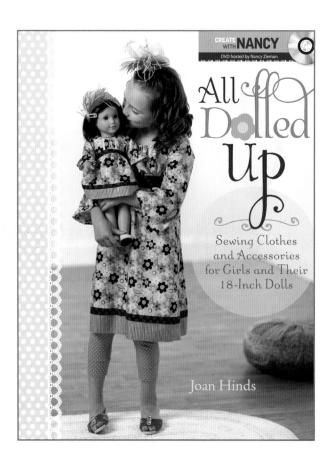

For 20 more great projects for girls and the 18" dolls they love, be sure to get a copy of *All Dolled Up* by Joan Hinds. From dresses to casual wear to accessories, you'll love these fun and lively projects! Don't stop at doll clothes—get great patterns to make matching clothes for girls!